INNER HARMONY

through

Mindfulness Meditation

Gustavo Estrada

Printed in the United States of America

First Printing, May 2013

ISBN 978-0-9891568-0-6

Published by Gustavo Estrada
gustrada1@gmail.com
http://innerpeace.sharepoint.com/
1231 Kenway Circle SE
Smyrna, GA 30082

The art on the front cover of this book, *Morning Sunlight*, is copyright by Dr. Akiyoshi Kitaoka, Department of Psychology, Ritsumeikan University, Kyoto, Japan. Dr. Kitaoka granted permission for its use on September 23, 2012.

In memory of my son Carlos (1968-2013),
a beautiful human being,
who fell victim to sectarian violence.

Table of Contents

VIII

Foreword

This book is about inner harmony and the actions we all must take—the cravings we should stop, the aversions we should release, the biased views we should let go—in order to allow the spontaneous appearance of inner harmony in our lives. We must not run after inner harmony; instead, we should remove all the barriers that block its entrance; our actions do not aim at attaining inner harmony but at eliminating its foes—cravings, aversions and biased views.

The essential ideas and framework of what is being presented henceforth come from two fields of knowledge, twenty-five centuries apart that individually and complementarily may assist inquisitive people in their mind-opening process. The first one, the practical side, consists of the well-documented teachings of a sixth century BC Indian sage, Siddhattha Gotama, better known as the Buddha, one of the first thinkers in history to discuss human suffering—the opposite of inner harmony—and to develop a strategy to eliminate such suffering.

The second source is the approach to social sciences known as evolutionary psychology, the application of evolutionary principles to the understanding of the human mind. According to evolutionary psychology, the mental traits of human beings are adaptations designed by natural selection in very much the same way as biological traits evolved in all living creatures. In other words, the evolution of mental qualities is an extension of the evolution of life.

Evolutionary psychology, the theoretical side, does not offer recommendations on the stopping of cravings, aversions or biased views. The reason to lean on some notions of evolutionary psychology is different. The evolution of pleasure's memories into appetites-cravings and of pain's memories into fears-aversions explains the nature of suffering, as the Buddha intuitively understood it. Neither Siddhattha Gotama nor any other person until Charles Darwin twenty-three cen-

1

turies later had any hint about biological evolution or natural selection. However, the extraordinary insight of the Buddha allowed the Sage to develop his strategy to reduce and eventually eliminate human suffering.

Regarding the first source, the Buddha's teachings [1] (the teachings, for short) are wonderful guides for living; for this reason, the Buddha's discourses are quoted extensively. Still this book is by no means about Buddhism and it cannot be so because some of its interpretations of the Buddha's thought deviate from what is generally accepted by Buddhist scholars.

The distance between this book and Buddhism is stretched out to even wider distances. Experiencing inner harmony does not require affiliation with any creed or endorsement from any religion, Buddhist or otherwise. Students need neither abandon their beliefs (religious or metaphysical of any kind) nor hold to them, whatever they are; beliefs are irrelevant and unrelated to the practices here recommended. This book is all about the application of common sense and has nothing to do with subscribing to or leaving behind any faith system.

The primary goal in this writing is to persuade readers about the soundness and logic of its contents. A more ambitious objective would be to motivate students enough so that they start practicing mindfulness meditation, an aspiration that is obviously more difficult to materialize because it demands the commitment of each individual. This author does hope, however, that effectively achieving the persuasive portion will push readers to undertake meditation of their own accord.

Besides the teachings and evolutionary sciences, there is a third component with strong influence on the book's content, namely the writer's own application of the Buddha's recommendations. Studying the teachings or learning evolutionary psychology is rational knowledge that people can gain from texts or courses; the Sage emphasizes,[2] however, that simply repeating (with no action) what we have read or learned by heart is as "counting the sheep of somebody else's herd" (or listing the merchandise of somebody else's store). This author knows the truth of what is here because of his direct experience with it; he understands that the application of the teachings does produce wholesome results, in direct proportion to zeal and perseverance. This realization became a driving force in the undertaking of this work.

But the experience of other people, however useful for them, is useless for the reader. This fact drives the writer to address the final emphasis of this foreword from the reader's side of the coin (as opposed to his own perspective). Though the wisdom of the teachings and the soundness of its practices are categorical, it is only through personal actions and real results that advice and discourse become truth for anyone. Only direct experience and actual observed benefits convince individuals about the effectiveness and profit of any procedure.

At times, this author refers to what is being presented here as Pragmatic Buddhism. For pragmatics, truth is what produces positive outcomes; whatever does not do so is wrong, false or questionable. Therefore, the teachings will only become true for people when they work for them as expected; not getting what a person anticipated from the application of a certain doctrine will make such doctrine false. Pragmatic Buddhism is exclusively personal and practical.

With much eloquence, the Buddha transmitted the direct-experience message to his contemporaries in a declaration that scholars commonly call "The Charter of Free Inquiry." This is one of the best-known statements of Buddhist literature:[3] "Do not accept anything because it is either tradition, generally accepted, written in some scriptures, based on logical reasoning, agreeable with your way of thinking or the word of a well-known master. It is only when you know for yourselves that some teachings are wholesome, and that, when followed and undertaken, conduce to well-being and inner harmony, that you should accept them, and live and act accordingly."

Chapter 1 – Inner Harmony

The Ideal State

Inner harmony is an internal state that permits us to be at peace and act confidently even in the face of difficulties. Inner harmony is not being in a good mood all the time; it is not ceasing to experience problems or the emotions associated with them. Inner harmony is neither the permanent show of a smiling face, nor the constant display of an optimistic posture. Instead, inner harmony is an evenness of the mind that, when troubles do arise, prompts our skills toward corrective actions, if they exist, or submits us serenely to the acceptance of reality, if problems actually have no solution.

Inner harmony is a worthy state of being—the ideal state—where most everybody would like to dwell. When we are enjoying inner harmony, we are living well. The paradox is, however, that we cannot move to such a wonderful state directly; we cannot take a particular sequence of steps that lead us there; we cannot *produce* inner harmony in a straight line.

Inner harmony is more the spontaneous result of a way of living than an intended, planned goal. People may look for things such as money, friends or academic degrees; these pursuits, though they may bring success, do not necessarily lead to inner harmony. Though inner harmony is quite different from success, the two qualities do not exclude each other. People enjoying inner harmony might be successful—they might have money, friends and academic degrees—but those things come to them naturally and they do not get frustrated if such effects do not arrive. To the eyes of others, they are successful; to themselves they are at peace with whatever happens in their lives. Inner harmony, which is personal and intimate, cannot come from outside; this would make it *outer* harmony.

We should not seek inner harmony; when we are chasing inner harmony, we are losing it. This paradox leads us to a challenge: If we should not hunt inner harmony, how do we get to experience it? How do we fulfill a yearning that we should not pursue? The answer is rather simple—though difficult to put in action. Instead of running after inner harmony, we have to direct our actions toward whatever disturbs it; inner harmony is a natural state from which something moves us away and to which we return as soon as we get rid of whatever that something is.

A Squeeze on Your Heart

The disturber—the something—that spoils our inner harmony is anxiety-and-stress. Throughout this book, we use this three-word phrase as a noun (as when we say *ins-and-outs* for the details of a situation, or *odds-and-ends* for miscellaneous items or pieces).

Defined separately, anxiety is the apprehensive uneasiness of the mind over an impending or anticipated event; stress is the mental state resulting from physical, job-related, social or financial factors that tend to alter equilibrium. In this book's vocabulary, the two words together represent what the Buddha called suffering and what he wanted to remove from humanity; the elimination of that suffering is the way—the approach, the strategy—to reach inner harmony.

There are many suggested English translations for the Buddhist word[4] equivalent to *suffering*[5]—anguish, anxiety, desperation, sadness, sorrow and stress. The Buddhist academics claim that none of these is accurate. As anxiety and stress are in their separate meanings, Buddhist suffering is predominantly a mental event.

Buddhist suffering encompasses all the nouns listed above yet it also goes beyond them. Suffering covers the uncertainty and difficulty that characterize all activities of life; since we can never be completely sure of an event's outcome, we experience anxiety-and-stress. With this extension, suffering includes the nervousness and apprehension involved even in

6

those activities that by their very nature are—or should be—pleasant or interesting.

We all know from firsthand experience that some positive and favorable situations, such as a new work assignment, the preparations for a celebration or the care and preservation of a romantic relationship, generate a certain level of worry that may lead to distressing and difficult moments. Nevertheless, in spite of being *acceptable* suffering, nobody would ever say that the new job uncertainties and increased responsibilities, the preliminaries of a party or the charm of a love journey are negative events.

Suffering is many kinds of mental loads. A story from Zen Buddhism describes a good example of such burdens. The story, which has numerous versions, goes like this: Two wayfaring monks came to a torrential creek where a beautiful young woman was standing, unable to walk across. The elder monk, without much thought, lifted the woman in his arms, carried her through, and let her down as soon as he reached the other bank. After walking for several hours without uttering a word, the young monk, very upset at what his companion had done, broke his silence: "We are not allowed to touch women. How did you dare to take her in your arms?" "I left the woman as soon as I crossed the stream," said the veteran monk. "You are still carrying her."

The anger of the young monk is nothing else but suffering. The mental state that the Buddha calls suffering comes from desiring what we lack (did the young monk want to carry the woman himself?) or rejecting what surrounds us (was it actually his companion's behavior that made him mad?). In either case, the young monk's inner harmony was disturbed; he was unnecessarily suffering.

Ajaan Maha Bua, a Thai Buddhist monk, provides a beautiful insight on the meaning of anxiety-and-stress in a short metaphor: "Suffering is whatever puts a squeeze on the heart." The list of issues that eventually squeeze our heart is indeed long.

The compound word anxiety-and-stress reflects quite well the meaning of (Buddhist) suffering. This book interchangeably uses either expression to refer to the same problem. Though anxiety-and-stress is a more accurate expression, suffering, being just one single word, is more concise. Either way, regardless of the word, if we want to eliminate suffering, we have to understand it—what it is and how it originates. Some sentences of the Buddha himself will prove most helpful in this direction. Who could provide better clarification than the first thinker in history who identified suffering as the fundamental problem of humankind?

Second Arrows

The Buddha continuously speaks about suffering throughout his preaching years; the following discourse encapsulates the meaning of suffering. In this story, the Sage compares suffering with what he calls second arrows:[6]

> Both unsettled people and people who live in inner harmony go through upsetting difficulties. They experience such difficulties differently, however. Unsettled people, when they face troubles, feel upset, as expected, and then they grieve, sorrow or lament, and become distraught and obsessed with what has happened to them; they first undergo the immediate effects of the problem and then move into a lasting feeling of anxiety-and-stress. It is as if an arrow hit them initially, which makes them suffer for a while, and a second arrow strikes afterwards, which makes them suffer enduringly.

> People with inner harmony, when facing troubles, on the other hand, they also feel upset, as expected, but just go through the experience of it; only one arrow hit them. They do not grieve, sorrow or lament, or become distraught or obsessed with what has happened to them.

They acknowledge the first arrow and adjust whatever is amendable. Second arrows do not hit people with inner harmony; they are not slaved by suffering.

First arrows constantly strike everybody. Bad things happen often to everyone: We all get hurt, have accidents, lose money, lose jobs or have disloyal friends. First arrows are real—we do sense their stings—and we cannot always evade them. Second arrows, on the other hand, develop and dwell in our heads. Second arrows are the enemy—the suffering—we want to eliminate or, at least, restrain.

Second arrows are the suffering of obsessive thoughts: "If only I had not done that; I should have driven slower; that crook is still out there; my boss treated me badly; my friend bad-mouthed me..." Such thoughts seem to have life of their own, take over our heads and disturb both our waking and sleeping hours.

Making things worse, we may have multiple second arrows, like dozens of uninvited visitors that take up residency inside our heads. Second arrows relate not only to bad memories we cannot let go; they also include the goods we lack but desire, and the things we possess or that surround us but we hate and want removed from our sight.

First arrows are normal; they come from our actual interactions with other people or from unforeseen events. Second arrows are imaginary and unnatural; they come from interactions of thoughts and memories within our heads. For example, the consideration to acquire something we find attractive or to move to a different, more pleasant neighborhood is perfectly natural; looking for something different is an acceptable first arrow. Obsessing over the desired change is a detrimental second arrow.

Suffering manifests as a wide range of mental events, from simple imaginary worries, through depressions and slumps in morale, to the most intense, evil bitterness. The intensity of suffering escalates—from simple worries to evil bitterness—

9

when our mind cannot liberate from adverse events or obsessive thoughts, and ruminates incessantly around them.

The Buddha is very specific in his definition of anxiety-and-stress, which appears in what Buddhist texts commonly denominate the truth of suffering.[7] The truth of suffering, the first of four declarations that constitute the summary of the Buddha's teachings,[8] states: "From birth, through aging and sickness, to death we permanently confront suffering. Association with the unpleasant leads to suffering; dissociation from the pleasant leads to suffering; not receiving what we want leads to suffering; getting what is not wanted leads to suffering."

Suffering as Feeling

Is suffering an emotion? Is it, rather, a feeling? There is a subtle difference between emotions and feelings; while emotions are the body's reactions to certain external or internal stimuli, feelings are the brain's perceptions of such reactions.[9] Suffering is a feeling; more specifically, it is a background feeling, a blend of several recollections. Some definitions are required to explain this subject, which will be covered soon.

The best-recognized emotions, the primary ones that occur immediately after a stimulus and without intervention of reason, are few: joy, fear, anger, disgust, sadness and surprise are primary emotions. The body's reactions to every emotion are rather specific, though they may change from person to person and, for the same individual, from one situation to another. Typical reactions to fear include racing heart, fast breathing, pale skin, contracted muscles or dry mouth. Responses to anger involve fist clenching, sweating, teeth display, skin reddening, voice rising or muscles tensing.

Feelings, in contrast, are the recording and processing the brain makes when it detects the body's emotional reactions. Only when our brain registers our heart racing, our fast breathing and so on, do we experience the feeling of fear. Only when our brain learns that we are clenching fists, sweating and so on, do we become conscious that we are angry.

As we are going to see later, this distinction is crucial to understanding the workings of meditation. The difference, however, may be difficult to assimilate because many feelings share the name of the emotion from which they originate, and emotions may vary in content and intensity. Furthermore, since feelings do not always come from emotions and we can experience *mixed* feelings, dictionaries have more words for feelings than for emotions.

Some examples might prove helpful to clarity. Primary emotions, like anger and disgust, lead to feelings with similar names. Still the emotion of joy may produce feelings of enthusiasm, excitement or optimism; the emotion of fear may precede feelings of panic, nervousness or anxiety; the emotion of anger may generate feelings of wrath, hostility or contempt; and so on. There are also background feelings (to be discussed next) that include mental states such as tension, relaxation or imbalance. The important point here is that emotional reactions occur in the body and feelings are *felt* by the brain.

While they are almost simultaneous, emotions precede feelings. We are not aware of emotions; we are aware of feelings. Feelings are the private, mental experience of an emotion; emotions are collections of responses to stimuli, many of which are publicly observable. Feelings are characteristic of human beings; animals do not experience feelings. Animals, however, do go through emotions; we all have seen angry dogs or scared cats. It is just that they are not conscious of being angry or scared.

Some emotions and feelings come from sensations, natural or incidental, pursued or unexpected. (Sensations will be covered in more detail later on.) In many situations, depending upon the intensity, the type and the source of the sensation, our brain processes sensations directly—no emotion between sensations and feelings. In any case, pleasant sensations might generate positive feelings such as joy, gratification or euphoria; negative, painful sensations lead to negative feelings like anguish, rage or annoyance. For instance, a soft tickling produces a feeling of euphoria, and burning our hand, a feeling of annoyance.

Feelings also arise with reminiscences of events that in their moment had emotional content. Our brains re-create these past events and tell the body to reproduce the related bodily reactions; some people even get upset just remembering unpleasant moments. The signals of these reactions go back to the brain and become feelings of sadness, joy or whatever.

Negative emotions and the feelings associated with them are first arrows; the negative feelings that keep coming back into our heads when we ruminate over bad memories are second arrows. Suffering is not a single isolated feeling but a background feeling. Background feelings are blends of emotional recollections and sensory signals that produce the general tone of life.

Suffering, as a background feeling, manifests differently from one individual to another and, in the same person, from one day to the next. The victims of suffering tend to deny, hide or ignore their distress and discomfort. While other people easily notice their misbehaviors (such as greed, arrogance or aggression) the *sufferers* consider such situations as normal, acceptable or circumstantial.

Background feelings darken or brighten our existence. Background feelings manifest in opposing duos: tension or relaxation, imbalance or balance, instability or stability, fatigue or energy. Anxiety-and-stress is a background feeling, described by tension, imbalance, instability and fatigue, the negative sides of these opposed duos; anxiety-and-stress echoes a combination of unpleasant sensory signals, bad memories and negative emotions.

Separately, anxiety and stress, the two words this book puts together to refer to suffering, are feelings that do not come from a single event or emotion. We all experience them at one time or another. It is only when anxiety and stress are chronic that they become background feelings.

Absence of Noise

If we cannot search for inner harmony—if we cannot walk directly toward it—what should we do to allow inner harmony to find us? We can begin by comparing inner harmony to silence. Both occurrences come from the absence of certain disruptions; they are not the outcome of specific actions. When there is noise in the environment and we are longing for quietness, we work on the sources of the distressing sounds: we turn off loudspeakers, end chattering and still motions. When the noise sources settle down, silence comes about.

Similarly, we cannot design or produce inner harmony; there are no instructions to build it. Instead, if we wish to experience inner harmony, we should work on the sources of the mental noise; we must attack and destroy the roots of anxiety-and-stress. But what are these roots? Cravings and aversions are the sources of anxiety-and-stress, the origins of the distressing sounds. Cravings and aversions are like loudspeakers the stridencies of which break off inner harmony; we must turn off the sound system if we want to stop the noise. When we eradicate cravings and aversions, the suffering they are producing disappears, and inner harmony blossoms.

Suffering and inner harmony run in opposing directions; the more we go through anxiety-and-stress, the less we enjoy inner harmony. Our enemy is cravings and aversions; our army is our body and our mind. An old Chinese classic of warfare[10] asserts that we should know both our foe and our militia if we are to succeed in a war. We must, therefore, understand cravings and aversions—our enemy—as well as our body and mind—our army.

The Chinese text also says that supreme excellence is seizing the enemy without fighting. Our combat against cravings and aversions should adhere to this non-struggling style; in our battle, we defeat the enemy more through restraints and passive stances than from actions and forceful motions. Inner harmony is the enduring flavor of victory every single moment we have cravings and aversions under control.

Chapter 2 – Cravings and Aversions

Pleasure, Needs and Appetites

Pleasure is a sensation of delight or joy. We well understand that definition because everybody has experienced pleasurable sensations. This is particularly true for the pleasure we feel through our touch, smell and taste senses; most everybody perceives contacts, odors and flavors in about the same way. At a higher level, the pleasure that results from sights, sounds and thoughts involves subjectivity and cultural influence; its enjoyment, therefore, might differ widely from person to person. In spite of perceived variations, human brains process enjoyment in the same way and pleasures tend to create appetites. Pleasure and the appetites it creates are survival mechanisms for every individual and every species; they developed in higher animals after millions of years of evolution and natural selection.

Pleasure and appetites drive creatures toward actions that favor the preservation of both their own life and their species' existence. When animals deal with a survival need, such as food or water, they experience appetites of hunger or thirst, the satisfaction of which produces gratification. These three events—appearance of needs, fulfillment of appetite, experience of pleasure—are a natural virtuous circle of slow repetition that generates well-being.

We inherited these mechanisms from our mammal ancestors. One of its wonders in humans is that the very search for the appetites' satisfaction is *deceitfully* pleasurable; this is why we *enjoy* the pains of love pursuits and the adventures of hunting even if the biologically associated need (sex or food) is not satisfied. In other words, the pleasing experience somehow begins when the cravings arise; natural selection made certain our remote ancestors did not give up easily.

In mammals, for we are such, the need to perpetuate the species awakens the appetite for sexual pleasure, an important driver for reproduction. Sexual appetite and sexual pleasure are as natural as the food appetite and its gratification; the sequence of events in the two circles—need, appetite, pleasure—is similar.

Pain, Threats and Fears

Pain is a distressing sensation that results from events that negatively affect the body of animals. After the body experiences a painful sensation for the first time, the brain registers the agent or the circumstances that caused such pain as a threat and programs an alarm signal associated with such danger—that beast is hungry, that river is torrential.

Later on, when the animal faces conditions similar to those that originally caused hurt, the alarm rings and its brain recognizes the threat; the creature then experiences the programmed fear and knows it should act to avoid the repetition of the pain. The animal quickly decides whether it should confront the problem or run away from it; the accumulated experiences build up its future fight-or-flight strategies.

As with the virtuous circle associated with needs, appetites and pleasure, the recognition of threats, the emergence of fear and the avoidance of pain also comprise another natural virtuous circle that repeats in the face of dangers to avoid or manage risky situations and prevent damages to our health. We humans inherited this second virtuous circle from our ancestors.

Similar to pleasure and appetites, pain and fears are survival mechanisms that favor the preservation of lives and species; more precisely, pain and fears drive animals away from dangerous encounters, situations or places that put them at risk. Though pain and pleasure work in opposing directions, they operate rather similarly in the nervous system of upper animals.

The similarity of the mechanisms of pleasure and pain in our nervous system might explain the enjoyment that many people experience in the practice of high-risk activities such as high-speed car or motorcycle racing, bull fighting and alpinism. Both mechanisms might share some nervous circuits that become confused in the performing of risky pursuits and the brain interprets the threats-fears of such activities as pleasant entertainment.[11]

Though we humans learn most fears by direct experience, we may have an innate fear of certain species, such as snakes or spiders; we can surmise that hominids and primitive humans that feared snakes and spiders had a clear survival advantage. The fear of death might also be natural in humans; we could speculate that primitives who were not scared by death took more risks and died young without leaving descendants. Our remote ancestors were the cautious ones who did fear death; they escaped more often from dangerous situations, lived longer and left more children.

The Top of the Tree

Throughout the ages, the species that handled biological needs and physical threats successfully and consistently were the ones that survived. The genealogical tree of life branched out in a million directions. Now and then, a limb withered and fell off—dinosaurs are the best-known example—but new branches kept coming out. Though the evolution of life moves very, very slowly, the tree never stops growing.

At the top bough of this huge, three-and-a-half-million-year-old hierarchy of life, there we, the *Homo sapiens,* are. In its upper portion, pleasure, pain, appetites and fears became the drivers that set the directions toward which the tree would grow.

Therefore, appetites and fears are normal traits of our human nature. They have specific roles and are fundamental for our survival—they sustain or save our lives at every moment. Pleasure and appetites provide information for our brain to manage our biological needs. Pain and fears do a similar job for our brain in the control of whatever threatens us.

Appetites and fears happen within us. The agents or means that satisfy our needs-appetites and the sources of our threats-fears, however, normally come from outside; our brain has no direct power there. If we want to understand needs and threats, then we should briefly cover the workings of our brain on appetites and fears; it is here that our brain has much influence and some control.

Excitation and Inhibition

Neurons are the nerve cells that make up the nervous system; they allow different parts of the body to communicate with each other. Neuronal circuits are ensembles of neurons that process specific kinds of information and manage specialized jobs.

Neurons communicate through electrical and chemical signals. Each neuron uses such signals to influence the activity of a neighboring target neuron or circuit. This influence is either excitatory—if it amplifies or facilitates the activity of the target, or inhibitory—if it decreases or suppresses its activity.

When it occurs for the first time, every learned or developed functional task—a piece of knowledge, a skill, an image, a recollection, a preference, a dislike, an emotional state, etc.—becomes a neuronal circuit. Every activity we perform and every experience we undergo results from neurons connecting together to form neuronal circuits.

Inhibition is as important as excitation. Excitation sends orders of action; inhibition transmits impulses of restriction. When we are hungry, some excitatory circuits make us search for food. When we are full, an inhibitory circuit tells us to stop eating. Similarly, when we sense a threat, some excitatory circuits make sure that we are frightened (our heart rate goes up, our breath rhythm increases...) and we take some action (face the threat, hide, get assistance or run away). When the threat is under control or disappears, some inhibitory circuit orders the frightening circuits to stop the confusion; panic fades and we relax.

At every moment, inhibition allows the execution by excitatory circuits of what is urgent and suppresses what is irrelevant; this means that inhibitory circuits must always be alert—must stay on permanently. Inhibition, however, is much more than an on-off switch. The role of inhibitory circuits goes beyond initiating or stopping an action in the target excitatory circuit; they also modulate (amplify or reduce) the intensity or degree of the action, in the same way as a control button increases or decreases the output volume of a sound system.

We do not need to understand the details of excitation and inhibition; the important points are the existence of specialized excitatory and inhibitory mechanisms in our nervous system, and the perfect synchronicity they must wield if our physiological functions are to work smoothly.

Virtuous and Vicious Circles

If things always worked as nature designed them, people would stop eating when they had had enough food and would never feel threatened by imaginary or unlikely dangers. Why do we overeat or get scared for no reason? If pleasure-appetites and pain-fears are natural, why do they not always function as evolution and selection designed them?

Let us begin with eating. Appetites, in their most basic expression, stem from our vital need for food; pleasure evolved by natural selection as a positive conditioner that drives the satisfaction of such need. The gratifying experience of eating conditioned our remote ancestors (including our mammal predecessors) to look for and consume food. We, modern humans, dutifully follow that conditioning every day.

19

Normal fears operate similarly from the opposite direction. Fears are signals of threats, such as predators, raiders or diseases, which may cause us pain; we know they produce pain because we have felt it directly or have seen it in others. The record in our brain of those previous events triggers such fears. Through the ages, pain evolved as a negative conditioner to do something—fight, flight or surrender—when threats appear.

The normal functioning of appetites and fears corresponds to the right design of nature. When this happens, needs-appetites-pleasure and threats-fears-pain are virtuous circles. These virtuous circles have embedded a sort of control that fittingly stops the whole process until a new need develops or a new threat appears. Unfortunately, our nervous system too often receives mixed signals. Some come from our own wrong decisions that supersede what the nervous system would do on its own; others, we receive from the environment.

On one end, we choose to eat more of those delicious, attractive portions though we have already had enough food. Perhaps we just want our stomach to be full in excess because we are anticipating long hours with no access to provisions. Maybe, unconsciously and non-stop, we are putting chips into our mouth during that entertaining chat, or some advertisements have seeded in us an urge to devour that tasty product ceaselessly.

On the other hand, we may pay much attention to repeated false alarms and permanent warnings, and go beyond sound precautions to avoid implausible harms, aggressions or sicknesses. Alternatively, perhaps, we cannot forget the painful experience we went through last year when we were right in the middle of that catastrophe or barely survived a car accident. The very thought that these incidents might repeat frightens us.

2. Cravings and Aversions

Our inhibitory circuits, confused by these behaviors or thoughts, often forget their duties and quit sending their controlling orders—stop eating because we have already had enough, relax now because the situation is safe—to the associated excitatory circuits; in fewer words, the normal control system stops functioning. The effectiveness of inhibitory circuits progressively deteriorates and, at some point, the problem becomes chronic. With nothing monitoring our appetites, we may eat until our body literally cannot take additional food. With nothing restraining fears, insignificant clues of danger or bad memories trigger imaginary threats every time.

When inhibitory mechanisms start working improperly, or stop working completely, the controlled virtuous circles (needs-appetites-pleasure and threats-fears-pain) become wild vicious circles. We cannot satiate our appetites, we keep enjoying the excess food, and the need for extra stuff does not seem to end. Alternatively, we cannot manage our fears; the memory of painful past experiences or the potential occurrence of imaginary dangers creates permanent threats in our head.

But with these vicious circles in command, the appetites for pleasure displace the appetites for real biological needs, and the fear of pain supersedes the fear of real threats. Awkwardly, the twosomes of appetite-pleasure and fear-pain then become the drivers of our behavior, and the actual needs and threats move to a secondary role.

When inhibition works properly, we experience natural appetites for food and sex, and natural fears for real threats. When inhibitory circuits deteriorate, such appetites become cravings—intense, abnormal desires or longings; similarly, fears turn into aversions—feelings of strong dislike or repugnance toward certain people or things with a keen desire to avoid or turn away from them.

Cultural Cravings and Aversions

Food needs and physical threats are not our only needs and threats. On our path to modernity that started ten millennia ago, we have opened the door to all kinds of new appetites and fears, which in turn become cultural cravings and aversions.

The continuous progress of the human society toward better ways of living has developed in us new kinds of needs for things such as possessions, power, fame, reputation or hobbies. With the appearance of these non-survival needs, we humans have substantially expanded the original, normal role of appetites.

In parallel with these new demands, we—the human race—also started to experience new expressions of satisfaction, which are certainly different from physiological pleasure. The joys that we feel when we obtain a salary raise or a job promotion, get a new home or car, receive a prize or honor, or buy the latest technological gadget are all examples of these non-biological pleasures.

The possibility of losing our acquired needs or not getting the desired ones—possessions, power, fame, reputation or hobby stuff—leads also to new varieties of threats that have no relation to survival. Furthermore, the actual loss of such conveniences produces a kind of pain which we easily associate with the physical pain that comes with survival threats. Moreover the agents that put at risk our contrived acquisitions or appetites (the boss that hates us, the competitor that outperforms us, the former friend who never calls back, the social group that excludes us...) become the targets of our aversions.

The appetites and pleasures of food and sex, and the fears and pains that come from physical threats are the result of the evolution of species, as discussed earlier. The same parameters, when connected with artificial needs and threats, are the product of the evolution of civilization.

Excitatory and inhibitory circuits manage these society-made needs and threats in a similar way. We might also experience *appetites* for surplus goods and possessions, lines of authority, recognition, accomplishments or hobby interests, and *fears* to lose them. Then when inhibitory circuits deteriorate, such peculiar *appetites* immediately become cravings and such odd *fears* transform right away into aversions. Unsurprisingly, these artificial cravings and aversions also lead to anxiety-and-stress, in exactly the same way as the biological ones, albeit at a faster speed.

Mental Formations

Cravings and aversions are mental formations.[12] Mental formations are all the behavioral routines—physical or mental—that we learn throughout our lives but mostly during our early years; after we adopt a mental formation, we may perform it just a few times or repeatedly for many years. The initial learning may occur voluntarily (we choose to acquire the routine willingly) or unintentionally (learning just happens). For instance, either we learn the lyrics of a song by repeating its lines keenly, or our memory catches the words with no conscious effort.

Each mental formation is a self-programmed neuronal circuit in our brain and corresponds to a routine. The neuronal circuit activates the associated behaviors either automatically with the occurrence of certain stimuli that we do not necessarily identify (we sing a song without knowing why) or deliberately from a conscious decision (we sing the song at a party).

Habits are good examples of mental formations. Sometimes we program them—the sequence to dress in the morning, the time and place where we have lunch; sometimes they *pro-*

gram us—the attraction of a potential partner that ends up in a love bond, the taste of a food that becomes our favorite.

The continued repetition of a routine changes it from deliberate choice to automatic reaction; every time the external stimulus ticks, we mechanically perform the associated behavior. This is how people eventually become masters in specific skills such as dancing, ball juggling or playing musical instruments. Our interest centers on *automatic* mental formations because they are the ones that shape and determine our regular behavior. This said, the expression *mental formations* always refers to the automatic ones.

Our brain registers both the stimuli that trigger every mental formation and their associated responses; these records are like instruction manuals. When we see that dishonest person (stimulus), our muscles contract and we get angry (response); when we smell that food (stimulus), our mouth salivates and we feel hungry (response).

Cognitive sciences do not yet fully understand the way our nervous system creates and manages the intricacy of mental formations. Neuronal circuits interact in puzzling networks to create new neuronal circuits of a higher level, together with progressively more elaborate mental formations that trigger a variety of responses to a variety of conditions; the diversity of combinations escalates and so does complexity. For the understanding of its relation with anxiety-and-stress, however, the simplification of the workings of mental formations, as presented in this chapter, should prove sufficient.

Mental formations are not good or bad—moral or immoral; instead, they are wholesome or harmful. The virtuous circles of legitimate needs-appetites-pleasure and legitimate threats-fears-pain are wholesome mental formations; the vicious circles of false needs-greed-pleasure and imaginary threats-dread-pain are harmful mental formations. As vicious circles, cravings and aversions are harmful formations; they are conditionings that generate abnormal needs or threats, and activate automatically in response to certain stimuli.

Harmful formations manifest in many ways. Examples include gluttony (unnecessary craving for eating), avarice (unnecessary craving for possessions), arrogance (unnecessary craving for importance), anger (sudden unnecessary aversion toward someone or something), hatred (continued unnecessary aversion) and resentment (continued unnecessary aversion toward something regarded as offensive). Quite on purpose, the word *unnecessary* is added in all the above descriptions to emphasize the discretionary nature of all these improper conducts.

Wholesome mental formations, on the other hand, often appear in behaviors involving moderation, detachment or absence of the same attributes or objects that characterize the harmful mental formations. Temperance (moderation of yearnings), meekness (absence of pride) and generosity (detachment from possessions) are examples of wholesome mental formations.

Every mental formation involves sensations. We do not crave foods, drugs or sex; we crave the pleasant sensations they produce. Similarly, we do not feel aversion for a certain person, a kind of event or a place as such; we dislike the unpleasant sensory signals or emotions we underwent with those people or circumstances in the past.[13] This connection between sensations and mental formations will prove crucial later on when discussing the importance of being aware of our sensations.

The Origin of Suffering

The recurring manifestations of one or a combination of harmful formations produce the blend of emotions, emotional recollections and sensory signals that lead to the background feeling of suffering; cravings and aversions are at the root of suffering.

If we picture ourselves in any of the states that come from the examples of harmful formations listed above, we easily associate anxiety-and-stress with these misbehaviors. We get sick (and overweight) when we eat too much; people isolate us when we are greedy, arrogant or resentful; we become the object of hatred when we hate; we feel tense when we are angry.

It is interesting to look at these mental states in light of the stories and metaphors quoted earlier to describe suffering. Anger and resentment are the suffering of the young monk after the senior monk carried the beautiful woman across the river. Resentments are the lasting feelings of anxiety-and-stress that come from the second arrows that should have never hit us. Finally, each one of the items in the list—gluttony, avarice, arrogance, etc.—are all squeezes on our hearts.

Cravings and aversions are, in summary, the causes of anxiety-and-stress. The Buddha states this fact in what he calls the truth of the origin of suffering. This truth, the second of his four, connects cravings and aversions with suffering as follows:[14] "The origins of anxiety-and-stress are cravings and aversions. Cravings are intense desires seeking something different from what we have or what we are; that is, passion for sensual pleasures and ambition for being something different than what we are. Aversions are intense dissatisfactions with what surrounds us or what we have now, or with what we currently are."

Mental formations are extremely important for two closely connected reasons. The first one, just mentioned, is the intimate link between cravings and aversions and the suffering we would like to eliminate. The second one, the sum total of our mental formations, the wholesome and the harmful, shapes our self—our sense of identity, the subject of our next chapter.

2. Cravings and Aversions

Our sense of identity, our *total* self, consists of two portions referred to as redundant ego and essential self; they do not have distinct borders and are not by any means black and white. Harmful mental formations, those resulting from cravings and aversions, build up the superfluous, artificial portion—the redundant ego; the balance is our essential self. (The words *self* and *ego* both refer to our sense of identity; *ego*, however, bears a contrasting connotation. While the word *ego* is used in reference to the surplus portion, the expression *redundant self* is avoided.) In the appeasing of harmful formations, there occurs an attenuation of the redundant ego and, consequently, a decrease of the whole self. These notions will be expanded in Chapter 12.

Our sense of identity is neuronal code of the highest intricacy level; its complexity—the complexity of this extraordinary mental software that self-executes, that is, it does not require an external user or operator to control it—is well beyond the current understanding of science.

Chapter 3 – Body, Brain and Self

Body and Brain

The body is the tangible portion of each one of us, the totality of our biological stuff—bones, muscles, lungs, hearts, nails, hair, teeth... Our physiology consists of a number of organic systems such as the respiratory, digestive and circulatory systems. Though all of them have very important roles, the portion that interests us now is the nervous system, the coordinator through electrochemical signals of everything we are and do in our lives.

The nervous system consists of a central system, located in our heads and our backs, and many thousands of peripheral branches, the nervous roads that reach every part of the body.

The central nervous system consists of the brain and the spinal cord. The brain, the central processing unit of our supersophisticated computer, controls all the other organs in the body. The spinal cord, the main connecting cable, is the pathway that links the brain with the peripheral nervous system. The peripheral nervous system is commonly referred to as the nerves. (The metaphors of computing technology used to describe our brain-body compound are very descriptive; still they entail considerable limitations and inaccuracies.)

The brain contains an extremely large number of neurons, the nervous system cells. Neurons use physical contacts with other nearby neurons to communicate with each other. Every neuron can send or receive signals from around five thousand of their neighbors. We have billions of neurons that altogether have trillions of conversation channels. Yes, our neurons and the brain as a whole are very talkative entities, well beyond imagination.

The electrochemical software stores the neuronal code that manages the totality of both our activities and the information required for their execution. Vocabulary, sentence structures and images as well as the instructions for every task and skill—everything we have learned, a lot of what we have forgotten and all the mental functions we can perform—are electrochemical records coded in our neurons and neuronal circuits.

This software set is not static. Acting on instructions from our genetic programs, the brain permanently develops new neuronal routines and new data files, as demanded by our survival needs, the threats from the environment, our preferences and decisions, and our style of life.

In parallel with the development of this huge number of instructions and the registration of an extraordinary amount of data, our brain also builds our most complicated program, the neuronal software of our *self*; the self is the union of aggregates (such as body and sensations) that constitutes our identity. Every mental formation we learn deliberately or we adopt involuntarily from the moment we are born is a brick in the structure of our self's *dynamic* building, an additional software routine in the gigantic software program.

The self is de facto owner of all the aggregates that make it up. We can say that our genome is the creator of both our physical *equipment* and our neuronal *software*, and that this neuronal software runs our life.

Two Identities

We humans live on two planes, quite different but intimately related: the first one is material and very tangible; the other is abstract and very subtle.[15] The material plane is our body, our physical characteristics—our hardware so to speak; the abstract plane is our self, our symbolic identity—the software that controls everything.

A symbol is something that stands for something else (as a flag represents a country), or that suggests something we cannot directly picture (as an *x* for an unknown quantity).

We can touch our laptop but we cannot touch the software that runs in it (though we well know when it is working properly, malfunctioning or inactive). Because it is symbolic, we cannot picture or touch our self.

When we look outward, we perceive through our eyes the physical individualities of other people, their bodies. We know about their existence because we can see them. Except in the extreme situations of deep comas, we clearly know when other people have died and their identities have ceased to exist.

When we look inward, we know about our physical individuality because we can also feel it—we see and sense our own body with much more intensity than the bodies of others. Furthermore, our brain perceives our self; the existence of the self in others we can merely extrapolate from our own experiences. Only each person is and can be conscious of his or her own self. When we die, the body disintegrates and the self ends; after death, there is no knower anymore. We cannot be aware of our nonexistence: "If I think, I am, but when I am not, I do not think, I do not know, I do not feel..." Only other people know when we cease to exist.

Our physical individuality and our body are equivalent entities; we take pictures of our face, a portion of our physical individuality, and place them in our ID documents. Conversely, the symbolic identity resides in our brains. In the complexity of the whole brain neuronal software, the routines that create and process the experience of self—our consciousness—are the hardest to understand and conceive.

The brain is part of the body; it is one of its many organs. However redundant the previous sentence may sound, it is quite common to talk about the body implying the *body ex-brain*. (We also do so at times when we want to make explicit the exclusion of the brain in a particular sentence.) We experience physical pain in the body ex-brain, though the brain is the central processor of the pain signals. It also happens in

3. *Body, Brain and Self*

animals since physical pain is not an exclusive human experience. All brained vertebrates experience pain and show it vehemently when it is intense.

Besides pain, we humans also experience suffering. Pain and suffering often come together and overlap with each other. Pain generates suffering, and anxiety-and-stress initiates or opens the door to diseases that bring about aches.

We come across pain through our physical body. The main territory of pain is our physical individuality and, under the management and control of the brain, pain happens—it is felt—in the body; the brain itself does not ache.[16] Suffering, on the other hand, is a mental event and its territory is the self; as we said earlier, suffering is a background feeling and feelings happen in the brain.

Aggregates of Personality

How does our sense of identity manifest? This author likes the interpretation of the Buddha. Our illusory certainty of a real identity, according to the Sage, comes from the five aggregates that characterize us as individuals and reveal through our physical and symbolic planes. These traits are (1) body, (2) sensory signals, (3) perceptions, (4) mental formations and (5) cognition.

The aggregates are manifestations of personality—the collection of physical, mental and behavioral qualities that provide us with the sense of being individuals. They do not depend on a machinist that controls knobs or a puppeteer that handles strings; still the aggregates do depend on each other and coordinate their duties, as do members of a sports team. The prodigious weaving and coordination of this dependence is what makes every person feel his or her sense of identity, what allows him or her to talk about *I*, *my* or *me*. Were this not so we would behave very similarly to other anthropoid apes.[17]

Our body, the first aggregate, coincides with our physical individuality, which is, we repeat, the tangible plane. The other four aggregates express through our nervous system that reaches every corner of our body. The second through fifth aggregates, though we can be aware of them, are invisible and untouchable; they are data and instructions in our nervous system and, at the same time, the makers of our self.

Body: The first aggregate is the totality of our external parts and inner components. Our physical body is the gross manifestation of our individuality. Our body performs all the visible tasks—walking, eating, talking, watching, etc.—that our brain controls and manages.

Sensory signals: The second aggregate is sensory signals, the bodily reactions to external or internal stimuli. External stimuli are optical signals, sounds, contacts, flavors or smells, which we receive respectively through our eyes, ears, skin, tongue or nose. The inner stimuli are bodily actions (such as innards' motions, aches or nuisances) or mental actions (such as directed thoughts, mind wanderings or emotional signals).

Sensory signals move through electrochemical impulses that permanently bombard our brain or explode within it. The sensory signals of mental actions occur directly within the brain; all other sensory signals travel from the body, through the nerves and the spinal cord, to the brain.

Perceptions: The third aggregate is the result of the brain sorting sensory signals. We constantly receive sensory signals—many millions of electrochemical impulses traveling through the nervous system to the brain or within the brain itself. If our brain did not ignore the large majority of these many electrochemical signals, their continual reception would overwhelm us. Instead, our brain selects for further processing a tiny minority of sensory signals about which we really do need to take some action. Perceptions, the third aggregate, are these reduced selections.

3. Body, Brain and Self

The relation between sensory signals and perceptions is similar to the one between emotions and feelings described earlier. Emotions occur as sensory signals throughout the body; feelings are perceptions and happen in the brain. In fact, the emotional body's reactions to stimuli generate sensory signals that travel to our brain; when the brain registers and processes them, emotions become feelings.

This book reserves the word *sensations* for the combined activity of sensory signals and perceptions. When we notice a sensory signal—when we perceive it, it becomes a sensation. We have already used this word with this consolidated meaning when we discussed painful or pleasant sensations.

Sensations result from all kinds of sensory signals; there are optical sensations, acoustical sensations and so on. However, the word *sensation* commonly refers to the sensory signals that we feel through the sense of touch.

Mental formations: The fourth aggregate was already introduced when cravings and aversions were presented as mental formations; the following paragraphs briefly review this important notion. Mental formations are brain responses that activate with the occurrence of specific stimuli; their programs, both the triggering stimuli and the responses, reside in our brain. The neuronal coding of mental formations comes from previous pleasant or painful perceptions. When sensory signals produce pleasant sensations, we want to repeat, prolong or intensify such events; when they produce unpleasant sensations, we want to avoid or at least reduce them. If we like a certain food, we want more of it; if we dislike a person, we prefer to stay away from him or her.

Mental formations mobilize our body toward desiring pleasurable experiences or rejecting unlikable ones. The pleasures or pains of an incident are the generators—the conditioners—of mental formations which will end up as drivers of our beliefs and behaviors. Mental formations are healthy qualities that are vital to our survival (food tastes good because we need to eat, hot objects burn so we should move away from them). However, they may also become harmful defects (we drink alcoholic beverages because they cheer us up; we hate someone because that person hurt us in the past).

Cognition: The fifth aggregate is the process of knowing, understanding, judging and being aware—our ability to call and use our knowledge, skills and memories—which can only be accessed by each individual; it is the storehouse where we keep both our library of everything we know, believe and are, and the instruction manuals for everything we can do.

The "consciousness" of our existence and individuality and our awareness of things within and outside us are capacities of the fifth aggregate. The faculty of awareness plays a fundamental role in both meditation and mindfulness.

Mind

The five traditional senses are sight, hearing, smell, taste and touch; their associated organs provide sensory signals for perception, respectively, eyes, ears, nose, tongue and the neuronal receptors located in several parts of the body, mostly in the skin.

Seeing is what our eyes and the eyes of animals do; smelling is what our nose and the noses of animals do; tasting is what our tongue and the tongues of animals do... "The mind is what our brain does," says Steven Pinker.[18] The sentence of this Canadian-American evolutionary scientist may be further demarcated: The mind is what our brain does and the brains of animals cannot do.[19] Mind is the complex of elements in our brain that senses, perceives, wills, remembers, reasons and is conscious.

We know that humans and chimps share around ninety-six percent of their genetic code.[20] The genetic instructions that lead to mind and self should reside then in that four percent of our genetics that our DNA displays and the chimpanzees' DNA lacks. That is the *little* big difference.

The Buddha considers the mind as a sixth sense, the organ of which is the brain.[21] Since perception occurs in the brain, the notion of mind being a sense implies that the brain is both the generator of some sensory signals (thoughts, divagations, recollections...) and the processor of such events' perception. The signals from the other senses, also processed by the brain, originate in body parts other than the brain itself (eyes, ears, etc.).

Whether the mind is or is not a sense is an issue that leads to controversies—neurologists do not even agree on the definition of *sense* and, consequentially, there is debate on the number of senses we possess.[22] However, the consideration that the mind is a sense and a product of evolution as the other five senses facilitates the understanding of the material origin of the self.[23]

In the ascent of life, the first five senses appeared very slowly, one by one; they preceded the mind, a relatively recent development in evolution, by eons. Billions of years ago, the first thing that rudimentary live entities did, other than copying themselves, was to perceive odors, that is, smell.[24] Progressively, in an extremely slow sequence, living entities might have been able to taste, touch, hear and see. Then, a few seconds ago in the timeline of life, humans appeared and were able to think and recognize their existence.

The mind, among its many functions, is the creator and processor of the self. Through millions of years, consciousness is the evolutionary reward to a quality that favors survival.[25] We can easily think of two remote anthropoid apes: one with some elementary hints of mental function, a bit of personal history or a very simple grasp of individuality, and another with no trace of mind, memory or sense of identity.

The first one, when facing a certain threat, not only experienced fear and made instinctive fight-or-flight decisions, as would any mammal, but also he or she could recall previous similar circumstances and reproduce actions that had already proved helpful. The chances of survival of the first anthropoid ape were higher than the odds of the second one; every success of the latter was exclusively aleatory.[26]

Once we understand that our mind is a product of evolution, we are in parallel acknowledging a similar nature—a similar origin—for our symbolic identity, its star product. However prodigious it is, our symbolic identity is a soft quality of our mind, a program that runs somewhere in our brain.

Materiality of the Self

For us, humans, it is difficult to acknowledge the soft quality—the subtlety, the intangibility—of our own self. We perceive our sense of identity so *grossly and solidly* that we refuse to acknowledge it as a neuronal software program.

Our physical individuality, the touchable and measurable body, is material substance that occupies space and has mass; our symbolic identity, the intangible and unquantifiable self, has no material substance—no atoms, no units of energy. The self, however, originates from the matter in our body and brain. Our self, the artificial impression of an entity, is just a super-complex piece of neuronal software that performs its work through the brain, the seat of our mind. The self comes from the body through its brain; our self has no matter, still it originates in material phenomena.

The self does give continuity to our behavior by providing a personal point of reference, which relates the events of the past (retained in memory) with the actions of the present (perceived as now) and the plans for the future (represented in anticipation and imagination).

Materiality is the characteristic of human existence according to which our self is the result of some neuronal software that originates and operates from our brain, and manifests through our body.

3. Body, Brain and Self

The perceived *solidity* of our self originates in the five aggregates of personality; none of them is the self but each of them contributes to the idea of a substantial essence. Symbolic entities (as the self) represent collective things, aggregates of materials that together become something new and different from the original components. For example, the citizens of a region make up a country; the players of some sport, when banded together, form a team; a group of birds compose a flock. The country, the team or the flock are different entities, respectively, from the citizens, the players or the birds; the collective entities present behaviors that are specific to the group.

Two further metaphors might help to visualize the emergent assembly. A pile of wooden logs, as those people stack by their fireplaces, is different from individual pieces. Logs are burned now and then, and new ones replace the old ones. There is nothing permanent in the stack; still it will always be *the pile*. Similarly, we can think of centennial schools. Nobody who was studying there the first day exists today; yet current students, teachers and employees, regardless of the buildings they occupy today, keep referring to the school and its name as a permanent entity.

Again, none of the aggregates of our personality is our self—neither the body (the physical individuality), nor the other four aggregates (the symbolic identity's components) taken independently or together. Still we feel that we are well-defined entities, with IDs, knowledge, relatives, loves, hates and possessions that seem some kind of owners of those things.

To recap, the materiality of the self, the symbolic identity that distinguishes us humans from other living beings, originates in material phenomena but it is not matter; the self is neuronal code and has no need of any immaterial essence within, behind or parallel to the physical individuality. The self is the subtle output of material processes.[27]

37

Impermanence of Human Existence

Impermanence is the quality of being transient and changeable. We know that our body, the aggregate of personality that we can touch and see, had a beginning and will have an end. Babies (we were one) are born and people die every day (as we will eventually). We also witness and learn about the births and deaths of members of other species all the time.

Temporality occurs at all levels. We know that within our body, new cells continuously replace the old ones that die; even those cells that are not replaceable (as most of our neurons are not) have the capacity to repair and regrow portions of themselves. Our physical individuality is in constant change. But what about the self, is it also impermanent?

The self generally provides the continuity of identity to the physical individuality but the self is not the body. We cannot match the self to the body; the patients of certain severe brain disorders, though they do have a body, lack a functioning self that we could consider the symbolic identity of that body.

Neither is the self any one of the other four aggregates. Sensory signals, perceptions, mental formations and cognition make up our mind, the *human software* that creates and manages our symbolic identity. We cannot assimilate the self, an abstract and intangible thing, to all or any of its four aggregates.

When the *human hardware* collapses, the *human software* does not have an alternative *machine* on which to run.[28] Because the self originates in material processes in the body, an impermanent entity, the self is also impermanent. We—both the body and the self—are, in consequence, temporary entities that will no longer exist after death.

The self, the neuronal software, provides continuity and consistency to a person's behavior, which manifests through his or her body. Continuity and consistency, however, do not mean permanence; we, the physical individuality and the symbolic identity, together and separately, are impermanent. Impermanence is the quality of existing temporarily and applies to everything in the universe, including all living beings (human or otherwise) and the universe as a whole.

Self and Suffering

How do the notions of mental formations, self and suffering relate? What comes first and what comes last? These issues require a recap of what has been discussed so far. First, cravings and aversions, the harmful mental formations, are the roots of suffering and the harsh enemy of our inner harmony. Second, mental formations, the wholesome and the harmful, make up our self. The answer to the latter question is that mental formations come first, then self and suffering follow; they both result from mental formations.

For different reasons, however, the self adds an extra dimension to anxiety-and-stress. At the instant of our conception and even nine months later, we humans are little beings with no sense of identity. Our self develops as we grow and age and, at some indeterminate moment toward which we evolve slowly over a few years, we start living in the two worlds we have described—a world of matter and a world of symbols. This duality involves the dramatic paradox of our nature: We are half-animal and half-symbolic.[29]

Our physical individuality disregards death. The possibility of dying does not concern young babies when their symbolic identity is still incipient. Animals, which do not know that death will eventually occur, feel no worry for their forthcoming demise. Beings that lack consciousness and capacity to think, that is, all beings other than humans, are not—cannot be—afraid of occurrences they are not aware will happen. Animals do instinctively become frightened and run away from imminent dangers; still they do not experience any long-term fear of death.

On the other hand, the mind that created our symbolic identity is also the mind that reasons; we cannot think of us being dead because when we are dead we do not think—in its actual meaning, the sentence *I am dead* is never pronounced. We see the body of other people dying and we perceive our own body when it aches or sickens, but our self can neither take its impermanence nor conceive itself as non-existing. Because of our symbolic identity, we humans experience either an illusory need to stay alive (a craving) and a fear of death (an aversion), or both; this combination of craving for life and aversion to death predisposes us to suffering.

The Definition of Suffering

The predisposition to anxiety-and-stress just introduced is an immediate consequence of our impermanence and our materiality. It is because of the two worlds in which we live—the physical and the symbolic, the biological and the psychological, the one given to us and the one that our mind builds—that we humans have such a predisposition to anxiety-and-stress, a third characteristic of human existence.[30] *Predisposition* should be underlined. Suffering exists but it is optional. Suffering is as real as bacteria, which are out there ready to infect us; however, not everybody gets sick.

The paradox of our dual nature resolves when we intimately understand—when we intuitively assimilate—the materiality of mental phenomena and the impermanence of all existing things. If we accept the materiality of mental phenomena, we truly know that our symbolic identity is a soft quality, not a parallel, immaterial entity inside or by our body. If we acknowledge impermanence, we know that everything changes and nothing in or around us is eternal.

So far, suffering has been described through synonyms, metaphors, stories, the Buddha's words and examples; now a definition of such word is timely. Suffering is the set of negative feelings generated by cravings for what we lack, and aversions to what imaginarily or actually surrounds us. What we lack may be things that we do not have at all, or things we already have but crave more of; examples include friends, love, money, food, power or prestige. The objects of aversion may be real people, things or events that actually surround us, or alternatively, imaginary threats or circumstances.

Addictions, Phobias and Extreme Suffering

Cravings and aversions are subjective experiences. Unless we display them openly, as when we eat disorderly or we express our dislike for someone at all times, very few will notice what the objects of our cravings or our aversions are. This changes when cravings and aversions grow in intensity and frequency; then, everybody will notice them.

As a specific craving keeps growing, our compulsive desire will show—we must have a drink—or the effects will be apparent—we are drunk. Though there is no clear-cut line, as cravings grow more demanding and persistent, they will eventually become addictions. Addiction is the state of a person dedicated or surrendered to something in a habitual or obsessive way. Addictions are more noticeable than cravings; eventually, they will also have an impact on our social environment or on our physical or mental health.

Similarly, as an aversion becomes more intense and frequent, it turns into a phobia, an exaggerated and usually irrational dislike of objects, situations or people. Panic in response to flight travel, repulsion to some insects and abomination for some people or places are examples of abnormal fears or fear-like emotions. Phobias may also be visible and can negatively affect our health or our relationships.

Like cravings and aversions, addictions and phobias carry suffering, in fact, extreme suffering. The mechanisms of the two sets of problems are equivalent: the malfunctioning of the inhibitory circuits. The extreme suffering generated by addictions and phobias usually hurts not only the addicted or phobic person but also his or her family, friends and coworkers; there it becomes extended suffering.

What we will be discussing about how to deal with cravings and aversions also applies to addictions and phobias. There is no such thing as a solid line that separates one set from the other; instead, there is a gray zone that grows dim with the degree or extent of the disorders. We can equate *mild to middle-range* addictions or phobias to intense cravings or aversions; what we say in this book applies to such ordeals. Obsessive-compulsive behaviors and mental ailments with genetic roots, on the other hand, are much more complex issues that demand specialized assistance.

Chapter 4 – Delusion

Opinions or Biased Views

Cravings are demanding mental formations; because of them, we desire a portion of something we lack, or a larger ration of something we already have. Aversions are rejecting mental formations—we want a smaller fraction or nothing at all of something we have and dislike. Whether we are greedy or resentful, the associated cravings and aversions are fetters that enchain us to suffering.

Cravings and aversions, however, are not the only chains that enslave us. The adherence to beliefs that cannot be established or confirmed is a similar fetter that also shackles us to anxiety-and-stress. These beliefs are opinions—biases or biased views.

Opinions are the broad range of prejudiced beliefs and bigoted views that lack backing from positive knowledge. We attach to opinions in a subtle way that makes them ours as if they were possessions.

As opposed to material goods, nobody can take our biased views away; even so, we defend them passionately: The more fervent our opinion, the harsher our defense. The problem with opinions—religious, political, racial or sectarian of any kind—is that they put a cloud between facts and us that obscures our understanding of reality, and alters our language and our behavior.

Basic cravings (for food, water or sex) come from biological needs; opinions, however, do not satisfy any organic requirement. There is no such thing as a natural opinion that we crave or reject by genetic design. Once some specific bias takes over our mind, however, we find interesting any thought that agrees with our acquired prejudice and we experience aversion to any opinion that contradicts ours. In the first case, we somehow *crave* for the company of those who share our opinions. In the second case, the holder of a clash-

43

ing opinion and even the very thought of such person become disgusting to us. Since the physical or mental *association with the unpleasant leads to anxiety-and-stress,* biased opinions will bring us suffering.

Opinionated people cannot recognize their contradictions or fallacies; their mental framework obfuscates their vision. They consider the color of the glass through which they see the world as the right one; you cannot explain green to someone who sees only yellow; his or her reaction will always be: "I do not understand how you cannot see the yellowness of my point of view."

Biased opinions are pervasive, harmful mental formations with quite a negative impact on the products of our thinking. Biased opinions deteriorate the quality of our conclusions more destructively than poor data or weak reasoning resources.

Poor data comes from ignorance or lack of knowledge: We do not know or do not have the information we need, or what we have is incorrect. If we use wrong information, our story is going to be wrong; if we add two inaccurate figures, the result is false and the calculator will not detect the problem. Regardless of how sharp we are, if the input we receive is faulty, the results of our evaluation will be useless—garbage in, garbage out.

Weak reasoning resources (resulting from below-average talent, anxiety or limited time for analysis), on the other hand, are the inadequate application of logic. If the math is incoherent, we will get erroneous totals. Perfect information, if we analyze it improperly, will produce incorrect results.

When we search accuracy and reliability, however, the damaging influence of wrong data or deficient logic fades when compared with the distortions that biased views create. A careful review of the proceedings of an evaluation, by third parties or by the person behind the analysis, will always detect any faults in data or logic. This is not so when we reach conclusions based on or supported by biased views. When this happens, we are unable to either recognize our own errors or take in any correcting advice. We consider right only those opinions that coincide with ours.

People seldom change opinion; the more biased the opinion, the more difficult the change. This resistance is particularly evident in the arena of religious or political beliefs. It is not so in hard sciences. Scientific viewpoints change often as knowledge progresses and investigators develop and validate new theories, which outdate previous accepted models.

People with different opinions will always have different pictures of the same reality; everybody sees the world exclusively through the mental eyes of his or her own opinions. Consequentially, *biased* opinions, not wrong data or faulty analysis, are the worst barrier to the truth in any field of knowledge.

Delusion and Suffering

Delusion is a persistent false belief held as true despite indisputable evidence to the contrary. Delusion comes from our attachments to biased views; they distort facts and lead us to accept inaccurate interpretations as trustworthy. The attachment to our opinions and the resistance to accept alternative paths lead to harsh disagreements and hostility; friendly relationships may turn into estrangement and animosity.

Eventually, delusion also leads to violence. Because we are so certain about our religious or political opinions, we try to impose them on other people—we want them to share the *truth* we possess. If those we are trying to convince have their own opinions, they will defend them against our intentions, with violence if necessary. Delusion makes us righteous and shuts any road to the acceptance of different points of view. Certainly, delusion leads to suffering; the more biased our opinions, the sooner and harder our suffering will be.

Why is it so difficult for us to change opinions? Better to ask, why do we not see the falsehood—the deceit, the fabrication—in our opinions? The rules to assess the veracity of any opinion are embedded in the neuronal code of our self; they become part of our way of thinking. It is as if in a sports match we had the referee not only playing on our team but also setting the rules of the game; our team's actions would always be the right ones.

For the self of any person, all the biased opinions it maintains are the correct ones. Consequentially, everyone's opinions are always the *truth* for their owners and only the actions or thoughts that go along with such views are right. The self always acts as referee and player: "Why should I change my opinions when I—my self, my mental structure, my way of seeing the world—knows they are true?" Blinded by their biased opinions, people will hardly consider alternative views and, even less, the possibility they might be wrong.

Chapter 5 – Mindfulness

The Path of Mindfulness

Let us summarize what we have covered so far. Life is difficult and its difficulties predispose us, humans, to suffering. Inner harmony, a worthy, desirable state, is the freedom from suffering. The cause of anxiety-and-stress is cravings and aversions. Furthermore, the attachment to biased opinions generates cravings and aversions and, therefore, it leads to anxiety-and-stress.

We should not hunt for inner harmony; we cannot aim at inner harmony as our immediate target. Instead, we should silence cravings, aversions and biased opinions. When we eliminate cravings and aversions, and liberate from the opinions that cause delusion, suffering stops. When suffering stops, inner harmony blossoms.

The last sentence in the previous paragraph is a rephrasing of the Buddha's third truth, which the Sage states as follows: "The liberation from anxiety-and-stress comes with the complete cessation, giving up and letting go, of every craving and every aversion. Inner harmony is the experience of the total, unconditional cessation of anxiety-and-stress." Inner harmony[31] is freedom from suffering.

As said in Chapter 4, biased opinions lead to suffering. We crave the association with whoever or whatever holds similar views (people, media or groups) and feel aversion to whoever or whatever holds opposing views (again, people, media or groups). In consequence, the end of suffering also demands the cessation, giving up and letting go of every biased view we hold.

At this point we know the problem—anxiety-and-stress; we know the roots of the problem—cravings and aversions; and we know what we will experience when we destroy such roots—inner harmony. What is there to do then? How can we destroy those harmful roots? We follow the Buddha's recommendation:[32] "Mindfulness is the only path for the overcoming of anxiety-and-stress, for the elimination of suffering, for the attainment of inner harmony."

Though later on mindfulness will be discussed in much detail, it is appropriate to provide two definitions of the word now: The first one is short and telling; the second one is more elaborate and descriptive. In the succinct version, mindfulness is the permanent awareness of life as it unfolds; this definition contains the full flavor of the meaning but it does not say much about the details on which we are centering our awareness or what else to do with our awareness.

The more detailed explanation follows: Mindfulness is (1) the active awareness of whatever we are doing, and (2) the passive awareness—the nonjudgmental observation—of our body, our sensations and our mental states. Active awareness is self-explanatory; it implies we willingly focus our attention on the task of the moment—we had better do so for the optimal execution of the task. Passive awareness, in contrast, demands some clarification.

Body, sensations and mental states are the first three foundations of mindfulness,[33] the domains or objects on which we should maintain our attention to gain freedom from anxiety-and-stress. Body and sensations are tangible, objective and rather stable; mental states are intangible, subjective and rather variable—they change over time. Our mental state at any moment is, broadly speaking, our answer to the question "how are you?"

In general, the tasks we perform have some goal (we have to obtain something that we, or somebody else, need or want) and require some agency on our side—our body does the necessary motions, our senses provide data on actions and progress and our mind, consciously or automatically, directs the whole thing. While active awareness centers attention on the stepwise process to obtain the desired result, passive awareness notices the sensory signals coming from our agency (from our body, senses and brain) as we perform the task.

There is bad news and good news in the long definition, which does not permeate from the short one. The bad news goes first. Being mindful, even for a short period, is a difficult endeavor or, better said, it is something we do not do regularly. During their peak performances, artists playing their instruments and sport stars playing their sports fully immerse in their activity and enter a state of mindfulness that positive psychologists call *the flow*.

Artists and sport stars are more the exception than the rule. Anybody who has ever tried to focus attention for five minutes on a static object or a slow-motion event (not on a movie or game) knows this well. The difficulty to pay close attention for a while comes from the ease and unruliness with which our mind wanders. We function mostly on *automatic mode* and seldom center attention on something for longer than for a few seconds. The perceived difficulty is such, however, that it discourages many people from the practice of mindfulness.

The reasons for mental digression originate in the myriads of sensory signals our brain must process every minute; they come from our body, our senses and the permanent activity within the brain itself. Fortunately, that processing is unconscious but, resulting from the neuronal *turmoil* and without *our authorization,* such signals quickly move us away from the main task we are performing.

There is also good news: Through the practice of meditation, we can increase—dramatically so—our ability to stay mindful; the task is feasible and we can certainly become more attentive for longer periods. We can indeed enhance our faculty of awareness. The process is challenging but straightforward: It is challenging because we should meditate intensively and regularly, it is straightforward because the instructions to meditate are quite simple.

Why Is Mindfulness Difficult?

In addition to the huge volume of sensory signals, the difficulty of being permanently mindful also comes from the way our self operates. The self—the neuronal assembly of our wholesome and harmful mental formations—manages us; that is, it manages our whole body, including the brain where both the mental software and our personal database reside.

The software of our self determines what we should do or avoid, what we should think or say, and how we should feel or react to external stimuli. Most of what we do runs automatically; we are less free than what we usually believe.

The neuronal programs, rather small when we are born, are dynamic and keep adding mental formations as new neuronal instructions. The additional code of what to do's and when to do's—the actions and the conditions that trigger them—incorporate in the whole system. As they shape our self, mental formations progressively become the decision makers for our behavior.

We commonly consider that the sphere of influence of our self mostly resides on our conscious territory and that, by utter power of will, we can bring everything to the surface and put our subconscious mind under control. It is not so. On the contrary, our subconscious mind, where mental formations act, is what sets the tone and defines the framework of our conscious activities.

The coding of new mental formations, wholesome or harmful, consolidates with the neuronal software of the moment, and the unnecessary cravings and aversions modify and become part of the neuronal code of the self. *Without anybody's authorization,* these extra harmful routines generate in our body-brain complex both useless superfluous needs and unwanted imaginary fears. In this process—extraordinary and hurtful—they give rise to anxiety-and-stress.

50

This artificial addition generates our desires to become different from what we are now, having more than what we already have, or being in a place different from where we are. Suffering is the recurrent thoughts—the uninvited sensory signals—of dissatisfaction that ruminate continuously in our head.

Our mind digresses all the time, even when we are sleeping—that is why we dream. Permanently, our brain polls the environment, our body and our memory in search of sensory signals that might demand intervention. Our inhibitory circuits stop most of the sensory signals; nevertheless, quite a few distract our attention. The brain records of mental formations contain the cues for all our cravings and aversions; when a sensory signal matches a cue, the associated craving or aversion comes into action, and our interest moves toward whatever the objects of our desires or rejections are. If we hear the favorite song of a loved one, there our mind goes; if we see somebody who looks like somebody we dislike, we recall whatever he or she did to us. This relentless mind wandering is what makes mindfulness so cumbersome.

How Does Mindfulness Help?

When a sensory signal, external or internal, matches the triggering cue of a mental formation, the brain generates the associated craving or aversion instruction. Since every mental formation connects, directly or indirectly, to a sensation, being aware of sensory signals, that is, maintaining attention on them, helps us take control. [34] The awareness of mental events weakens the automatic operation of the self.

For this to happen, there should be no fight or resistance against such mental events; awareness must go together with a nonjudgmental acceptance of such events, exactly as they are. We have to remember that sensory signals and emotions happen (mostly) in our body and all perceptions and feelings occur in our brain, where the program of our self resides.

Our active awareness takes notice of what we are doing and our passive awareness remains attentive of what is going on within the brain and throughout the body. While this is happening, who is aware and who is accepting? These questions will be discussed later on. For now, it is important to point out that through mindfulness the harmful mental formations give up much of their power.

The awareness of the biased views that lead us to delusion operates similarly. With the impartial observation of the framework of our beliefs, that is, with the close examination of the opinions that support our way of thinking, the clouds of delusion fade away.

Acknowledging Anxiety-and-stress

We do know that suffering exists; everybody has something to say about anxiety-and-stress. Books, sayings and stories about suffering abound; they are of all kinds—well intended, religious, inspirational, cynical, humorous... Most of them, however, are impersonal and seldom speak explicitly of the experience their authors are undergoing. (Artists are one of the few exceptions to this trend.)

Most people are reluctant to acknowledge their suffering; either they claim to be happy and balanced, or do not see their anxiety-and-stress as a problem. American philosopher Henry D. Thoreau disagrees; he writes,[35] "The mass of men lead lives of quiet desperation. What is called resignation is confirmed desperation." Still if a person does not recognize his or her anxiety-and-stress—its reality, its detriment—such person has no reason to take any corrective action; we cannot solve a problem we do not admit exists.

People deny their anxiety-and-stress simply because they think they are in command of their mental states (nobody wants to accept that he/she is not the master of his/her life), or consider their existences are beyond good and evil; both positions provide a fitting sense of security. Such attitudes are respectable in every sense; each person experiences and judges their inner world, and only they can recognize the presence or absence of noises or problems in their mental states.

Borrowing the words of Indian philosopher J. Krishnamurti, this book invites all those comfortable readers to observe, very carefully, "the contents of their own mind and the mirror of their relationships." What is in there? Is it patience or intolerance, harmony or anxiety-and-stress, serenity or desperation? Only each person, again, can answer those questions. Honest, sincere answers will confirm their certainty—yes, they are patient, harmonious, serene individuals who are beyond suffering—or will show them their faults—they are intolerant, stressed, anxious people who might need to take some corrective action.

In the first case, they might have arrived to equanimity and inner harmony through other roads. That is wonderful! Alternatively, perhaps they might be one of those few who, blessed by nature or nurture, do not experience cravings or aversions. They are the lucky ones! There are indeed egoless individuals by a fortunate convergence of in-born predisposition and environmental circumstances; the two conditions together forge special beings. In the second case, the perception of clear signs of intolerance, hostility, anguish or other negative feelings will show them that there are problems to solve, and that mindfulness might be a helping alternative.

Since the ravages of anxiety-and-stress are the exclusive experience of the victims, they, and only they, can assess the benefits of stopping suffering. What are the costs of such a decision? Both continuous mindfulness and the permanent practice of meditation demand commitment; this is the investment to make.

Investors know that, when the potential benefits of a venture are substantial, the motivation to put money in is high. Similarly, once we acknowledge suffering—our suffering, the disturber of our inner harmony—we have sufficient good reasons to consider and try mindfulness. On top of acknowledging anxiety-and-stress, we must also understand cravings and aversions as the roots of problem; these roots are what we must destroy to reach our main goal.

Where are we now? We know that (1) mindfulness is the path to end suffering and enjoy inner harmony, (2) being mindful permanently (or even for short periods) is a demanding task and (3) the practice of meditation will increase our ability to be mindful. In other words, we have a very worthy endeavor—the cessation of anxiety-and-stress—that demands the commitment to meditation, which, in turn, helps us to stay mindful for longer periods. The significant returns of the project plainly justify the considerable investment.

Inner harmony is the beauty—the attractive return—that suffering is blocking from us. When we are really acquainted with our anxiety-and-stress—what it means and how it damages us, the considerable determination our battle demands will look feasible and manageable. Our decision to fight suffering becomes easier at the very moment we acknowledge *our own* anxiety-and-stress, the one we directly feel, not the suffering of the other, of the rest of the world. Once we intimately understand the magnitude of the problem—the elimination of which is the return on our investment, we will be ready and willing to undertake the project.

If mindfulness is the path, meditation is the assistant that helps us to reach our destination; the word has been used several times up to this point with no further clarification; the time has come now to cover this theme in detail, so *meditation* is the subject of the next chapter.

Chapter 6 – Mindfulness Meditation

Meditation

Meditation refers to a broad set of physical and mental exercises through which their practitioners manage and control their attention in search of certain benefits such as stress reduction, health improvement, spiritual growth or performance enhancement. Mindfulness meditation,[36] the approach that interests us, is an approach to meditation that, from the perspective of the ease and comprehensiveness of its instructions, is the simplest one.

There are many kinds of meditation; they may be part of behavioral therapies, religious rituals or personal growth routines. On the physical side, the diversity of techniques results from whether meditators remain static or move around; are sitting, laying or standing; stay quiet or utter some sounds or words; or keep eyes closed or open. On the mental side, the number grows substantially from the approaches adopted for attention control. Much trimming is needed to reduce *general* meditation to *mindfulness* meditation.

The top-down approach to excluding the unwarranted variations is two steps. In the first one, meditation is circumscribed to a specific practice that follows four widespread guidelines. In the second step, the word is further restricted to a very specific kind of meditation technique.

The guidelines of the first step are:[37] (1) the meditation session takes places in a quiet environment; (2) meditators adopt an open passive attitude; (3) meditators sit in a comfortable posture and (4) they manage and control their attention by focusing it on specific objects or anchors. The quiet environment, the passive attitude and the sitting posture exclude from our scope of the word *meditation* a number of exercises such as tai chi, hatha yoga, walking meditation and ritual dances.

The overall aim of meditation is to put at rest or, at least, to slow down as much as possible, the activity of the six Buddhist senses—sight, hearing, smell, taste, touch and mind.

Let us deal first with the *standard* five senses. The environment (item 1) for the practice—quiet, preferably dark, fragrance-free—should cut off most visual, auditory and olfactory digressive signals. Item 1 settles down the senses of sight, hearing and smell. The passive attitude (item 2) demands inaction; it implies, among many other things, the refraining from eating or drinking, which suspends or reduces the possibility of taste signals. The passive attitude also involves a nonjudgmental attitude toward distracting thoughts, which, together with the focusing of attention (item 4), helps in the appeasing of our mind.

The comfortable posture (item 3) aims at stillness. An easy posture should allow the practitioner to stay motionless for a long period, which minimizes touch contacts and body sensory signals. Sitting may be on the floor, the recommended and most common option, or on a chair, an acceptable alternative for those people who cannot tolerate sitting on the floor; uneasy, distressing postures tend to become achy and force meditators to move. When meditators feel forced to move about for any reason, they should do it slowly and silently. The abstention of foods for at least two hours before starting the practice is also appropriate; this short fasting reduces the innards' motions of digestion during the meditation period.

The mind, the sixth Buddhist sense, and the brain, its associated organ, come next. In our alert hours, our mind—the mad fellow in the attic, as some people call it—never stops running; even during sleep the mind does house cleaning of its files and engages in dreaming. The reality is that thought just happens and we do not choose the subjects of our wandering; they simply emerge.

The mind takes its attention-deviating inputs from two sources. The first one comes from outside the brain, from the five conventional senses, the activity of which the practitioner should have already slowed down through the application of the first three items of the meditation guidelines.

The second input is the mental actions—thoughts, digressions, daydreaming and so on—that spontaneously originate within the brain itself. Harmful mental formations, with no control on our side, are common suppliers of seeds for distracting thoughts; the objects of our cravings and aversions often pop up in our head without permission. This is where attention control (item 4) enters the game. Furthermore, it is where mindfulness meditation differentiates largely from many other types of silent, sitting, passive techniques.

We cannot stop uncalled thoughts; however, we can become aware of them, or we can switch our attention to an object of our choice and put distractions on hold. Meditators may use either of these two approaches. In the second approach, the objects on which meditators focus their attention are like the anchors that hold ships in place.

The anchors for mindfulness meditation are the second step (the general guidelines were the first step) to circumscribe the meaning of the word *meditation* to a reduced set of easy-to-apply, straightforward techniques.

Selection of Anchors

What kind of anchors should we use to focus our attention? Let us begin with exclusions, the list of objects that mindfulness meditators *should not* use. Though several of the items that follow have proved useful for many people, they are not appropriate anchors for mindfulness meditation. The list of exceptions is long to emphasize the difference between the two broad groups of techniques—mindfulness meditation versus other approaches.

The anchors not to use, some of which are well known in personal growth movements, include verbal or mental repetition of words (mantras), background music or chants, counts of beads in rosaries (malas), colored figures as circles or squares, concentric diagrams (mandalas), mental recalls of beautiful scenarios and images of teachers or saints.

While these anchors might work for focusing attention, they have several faults. First, they invoke unnecessary sensory signals—mental, auditory or tactile—that increase brain activity instead of appeasing it. Second, they are artificial, arbitrary and demand confusing choices (for example, which mantra to use, what chant to sing, what music to play or what color to select). Third, some items, such as the use of rosaries or the action of singing, require motions, however subtle, that run against stillness.

Finally, and this is their most significant weakness, the unconscious association of these devices with the pleasant experience of meditation leads to unwelcome cravings—new mental formations—that eventually create dependence from such ritualistic anchors.

This author does not mean to ban these meditational approaches; as long as they do not become fetishes or lead to fanaticism, they are better than not meditating at all. If practitioners are getting some benefits from the use of these artificial anchors, they might keep applying them; however, this partial success will keep them from trying mindfulness meditation (which is a further shortcoming of these anchors).

The anchors covered so far are the inappropriate ones. What shall we use instead? There are two broad categories in the approaches to mindfulness meditation, which parallel the first two items of the foundations of mindfulness, the objects for developing and maintaining our ability to stay mindful as long as possible.

6. Mindfulness Meditation

The first category corresponds to anchors around the body and some of its functions; the second one centers attention on the sensations throughout the body. These two sets of anchors are everything meditation students need to know and use in their practices; their simplicity is what makes mindfulness meditation, from the perspective of its instructions, the easiest meditation technique.

With anchors around our body or our sensations, there is no room for interpretation or analysis, or any particular need for advice from teachers or experts—we know our body, we feel our sensations; we have direct experience of these kinds of anchors. (Mental states, the third foundation of mindfulness to be covered later, are by their own nature a much more subjective set of items; this book does not recommend their use as anchors for meditation.)

For both body and sensations, their application as anchors may be through focusing on a specific spot, or by rotating attention—alternating consecutively the body parts to which we are directing attention or at which we are feeling sensations. For the fixed approach, meditators focus attention on one single item, for example, their breath as it enters and leaves their nostrils, or the sensation we perceive at a particular point. In the rotating alternative, meditators move attention around to observe (just to observe) the body's different parts, or rotate attention throughout the body to become aware of (to notice with no judgment) whatever sensory signals they perceive.

The body-sensations duo not only provides a framework for the anchors to use but also defines the best sequence the students should follow over time in their practice. This means that new students may want to start meditating with their attention focused on their body and, being more specific, on their breath. Then, as they gain experience, they move their practice to the observation of sensations. Appendix 2 contains the Buddha's guidelines for meditation using breath and sensation as anchors.

The Essence of Mindfulness Meditation

In the previous sections, mindfulness meditation has been circumscribed with a top-down selection—from meditation, in general, down to the technique the Buddha recommends; it is timely now to recap the essence of this practice in its basic approach. Mindfulness meditation is a mental exercise during which practitioners with their eyes gently closed, sit in a comfortable position in a quiet environment, adopt a passive attitude and focus attention on certain anchors in order to enhance their daily awareness; whenever meditators notice that their attention is off course, they take it back to the anchor of their choice. The two most commonly used anchors in mindfulness meditation are our breath and our sensations.

Level zero is the expression this book uses to refer to the mental state meditators reach when they abide for a long while (for example, forty-five minutes) to the above definition; this *level zero* expression will be repeatedly used in later chapters. When somebody meditates frequently (several times per week) and stays in level zero consistently, he or she is a *regular* meditator, a short step beyond a new student or beginner.

Both the holding of focused awareness and the return to the anchors in use when attention is astray are key elements of the practice. During meditation, we should not only maintain attention on our anchors but also detect the escape of the attention to a different object or event.

Mindfulness implies both active awareness of the task of the moment and passive awareness of the sensory signals from the body, sensations and mental states; digressions normally originate in these signals. By focusing attention during meditation, we are training our active awareness (the awareness of the activities of our conscious mind); by detecting distractions and pulling attention back to anchors, we are training our passive awareness (the awareness of the motions of our subconscious mind).

(From this point on, *meditation* with no qualifiers denotes mindfulness meditation. If a reference relates to other meditation approaches—as done a few times—it will be so specified.)

Body and Breathing

Our body provides the first set of meditation devices. Within the possible alternative anchors in our body, our breath is the most appropriate and common to apply; in fact, some meditators use their breath as the exclusive anchor of attention for their practice. Focusing on our breath is also the best way to begin the training practices when we are learning meditation and a good starting point for our daily sessions.

Breathing connects us to life so intimately and permanently that we cannot stop such a vital function for longer than a few minutes. Though we seldom do it, we can become aware of our respiratory activity—whether slow or fast, steady or irregular, deep or shallow. In contrast with breathing, for example, we cannot easily (and we do not need to) focus attention on other vital functions that also involve motions (such as our heartbeat or the flow of blood through our body's circulatory system).

Focusing attention on our breath is the best and easiest-to-explain technique of mindfulness meditation; it is also, by far, the most common meditational anchor of many traditions. "Be present at every breath; do not let your attention wander for the duration of a single breath" is well-intentioned advice that followers of both Islam and Hinduism attribute to masters of their religions.

Given that we are seldom aware of our breathing motions and the flow of air through our nose is quite tenuous, how do we focus our attention on our breath? If breathing is such a natural activity, what is there to observe?

We pay attention to very simple things: Is air flowing in? Is air flowing out? Are exhalations long? Are they short? We are not trying to change or add anything to the breathing rhythm. We are just aware of the breathing as it happens; we observe a body that is breathing; we notice that, through the nostrils, there is some air entering naturally and there is some air exiting naturally.

Every now and then—sometimes every few seconds, sometimes after minutes—attention escapes; for a while, we do not even notice it is gone. Our mind goes somewhere else and we do not even realize we are wandering. At some point, we take note that our mind is up in the sky, and we return attention—we pull the mind down—to our breath, with no judgment or frustration for our distraction.

If it so happens—if we do get judgmental or frustrated, we have only to skip such thoughts and redirect attention to our breath. If we feel glad because we are doing well, again, we just ignore our gladness and send attention back to our breath. If we wonder about the length of the exercise—for how long we have been sitting, how much time is left, what we shall do next—we refocus attention on our breath. We repeat the *landing* routine whenever we get bored, anxious, hurried, lost in ramblings...

Becoming aware of inattention is the beginning of awareness. Catching our mind wandering is a crucial step in the whole exercise; it means we are doing it right: The more often we have to return attention to our breath, the more attentive we are becoming. This back-and-forth is a *standard* procedure of the practice.

The excessive repetition of cycles of distractions-comebacks should not discourage meditators; every time we pull down attention to the anchor in use, we are strengthening attention. The capture of our volatile mind, as soon as it loses track of whatever we are doing at any moment, is also key to staying mindful during our common hours.

6. Mindfulness Meditation

The voice of an instructor or a soundtrack that periodically repeats a sentence like "maintain attention on the breath" will prove very helpful for beginners and cannot be damaging for experienced practitioners.

After a few sessions following live or recorded instructions, students should be able to carry on the practice with no external assistance. However straightforward meditation seems, there is never too much emphasis on the commitment and will that students must apply if they expect to become habitual meditators.

After students have tried a routine, something similar to what was just described, for a few days or weeks, two extreme things—or many combinations in the middle—may happen. The bad case is that they reached only a very *few days* and gave up the practice rather quickly; the only advice here is to go back and keep trying. The best scenario is that their sessions became an effortless habit and they keep meditating daily.

Many new students end up in the first group; the worst case is when people do not even dare trying meditation at all. Setting aside time to meditate every day and sitting in silence for a long while are challenging endeavors. Difficulty and resistance, however, go sharply down with practice; the more we meditate, the easier meditation becomes.

There is further good news for those who persist. If students are comfortable with the practice of centered-on-the-breath meditation, they may well stay there; this is a universal meditation technique. The use of anchors around sensations, to be covered next, is an excellent complement that provides variety to the meditating experience; the availability and use of alternative techniques is very important for many meditators. The above comments on distractions, judgments, frustrations, recorded or live instructions, flying-solo and persistence apply to all types of meditation routines.

There are additional approaches for meditation around the body parts and functions, as well as around sensations. Still, focusing on the breath superbly does the job of developing our mindfulness skills—our faculty of awareness.

Sensations

The second set of meditation techniques centers on sensations. A sensation is the perception of a sensory signal either because the brain decides that there is something to do with it or we intentionally direct our attention toward the associated stimulus. The feeling—the detection—of a sensory signal makes it a sensation.

A sensation begins when stimuli trigger sensory signals on a sense organ and completes when the brain processes it. There are many kinds of sensory signals and sensations—visual, acoustical, olfactory, touch, thermal and dynamic, among others. Sensory signals occur throughout the body (most of them) and within the brain (the mental ones); perceptions occur in the brain.

Our consciousness ignores the large majority of sensory signals that sense organs send to the brain (including the signals the brain generates and circulates within itself); we do not need to know about them. For all purposes, these signals do not seem to be happening.

Good examples of sensory signals to which our consciousness pays no attention are skin contacts with our clothes or the chair where we are sitting; we do not feel such contacts, unless we direct our awareness to the areas where they touch our skin or if they are extreme sensations, such as too comfortable chairs, itchy sweaters or tight shoes. Certainly, thousands of sensory signals never reach our consciousness—we could not perceive them even if we wanted; for instance, we cannot feel the majority of sensory signals related with our physiology, such as blood circulation, digestion or joint motions.

When we use sensations as anchors for meditation, sensations apply to the six Buddhist senses. The four guidelines of meditation, however, aim at reducing—when not cutting off—the sight, hearing, olfactory, taste and mental sensory signals. Because of this reduction of scope, we can safely restrict the meditation practice to touch sensations; *touch* here includes not only skin contacts but also all other sensory signals we perceive throughout our body and inside it (such as heat, moisture, dryness and tingling) as well as body motions (such as heartbeats and belly in-and-outs).

Touch sensory signals travel from all parts of the body, through the nerves and the spinal cord, to the brain, which chooses to perceive a fraction of them. Touch sensations are like a bridge between body and mind.

Sensations can be categorized from two perspectives. On one hand, sensations are unpleasant, pleasant or neutral; on the other, they are gross or subtle. Gross sensations are generally unpleasant or neutral, while subtle sensations are generally pleasant or neutral. These denominations are subjective and not critical at all. What is gross for one person might be neutral or subtle for another; they will never be able to tell the difference. Some hints follow anyway.

Gross sensations are either those we would feel even if we were not meditating (e.g., a headache or a cramp) or those we perceive when we direct attention to contact points on our skin during meditation (e.g., the contact with the chair or floor). Gross sensations are solid, apparent, downright and continuous. Subtle sensations are just that... subtle, hard to notice, rather difficult to explain and generally discontinuous; they come and go.

These categories are far from black and white—the threshold of pain and the perception of pleasure change widely from person to person. The purpose of this labeling is to provide some clue as to how to focus attention: When we feel a pleasant sensation, we mentally repeat, "this is a pleasant sensation"; when we feel an unpleasant sensation, we mentally repeat, "this is an unpleasant sensation"; when we feel a neutral sensation, we mentally repeat, "this is a neutral sensation."

It is advisable, as already mentioned, to start meditation sessions by focusing attention on our breath. After a few minutes, practitioners may scan their body in search of sensory signals. When they perceive one, which makes it a sensation, meditators simply acknowledge its presence and observe it with no judgment—whether it is painful, pleasant or neutral; whether it is subtle or gross—and keep on with the scanning process, in search of further sensory signals. In this approach, sensations follow attention—meditators move attention and sensations may (or may not) show up.

It may also happen that *some sensations call for attention*. As a common, non-meditation example, this so happens when an itching, scratch-demanding gross sensation arises. Though itching may also happen during the actual practice, the meditation sensations are commonly subtler—they may be so subtle that, if we were not meditating, we would not feel them at all. Meditators direct attention to where they perceive the fresh sensory signal, observe it and wait for the call of another sensory signal that *wants to be perceived*. In this approach, attention follows sensations.

When digressions occur (and they will occur repeatedly), the practitioners should pull attention down, either directly to search and observe sensations, or to the breath and the flow of air in and out of the nostrils.

Students might choose to scan freely their whole body for sensations, in whatever sequence they prefer; gross sensations always show up first. When there is no perception of any sensory signal in some area of the body, students should just be impartially aware of that part of their body and that there is no sensation there.

The awareness of blank insensible portions—blind spots—somewhere in the body is part of the exercise of awareness; awareness of the body is meditation on the first foundation of mindfulness. There should be no concern about quantity (too many, too few, none...), variety (gross or subtle, pleasant, unpleasant or neutral), nature (heat, cold, dryness, wetness, tingling, itching...) or intensity (slight or manifest). The training of awareness is what matters.

Breath and Sensations

The instructions to focus attention on our breath as it enters and leaves the nostrils are straightforward; some people might consider them hard to follow but no one can judge them difficult to understand. Similarly, focusing or rotating attention around gross or contact sensations leaves no room for doubts but again staying attentive to sensations might prove hard for new students.

On the other hand, the description of subtle sensations is fuzzier. Subtle means, by definition, well, subtle—slight, fine, weak... Conveying the feel of subtle sensations is as blurry as explaining flavors. Some beginners experience and recognize subtle sensations soon after they start their practice of meditation; other people may require many hours of patient sitting, focusing attention on their breath, before perceiving them. As we should not pursue inner harmony, we must not go after subtle sensations; such an endeavor will frustrate meditators and discourage them from their practice. Eventually, every practitioner will perceive unambiguous, subtle sensations.

These subtle sensations are generally pleasant, yet students should not try to find or *invent* them; they are real sensations and eventually will show up. When this happens, the meditation practice becomes a pleasant experience; boredom will no longer be an excuse for not meditating. Nevertheless, in the practice of meditation, students should neither look for any kind of pleasant experience nor struggle to avoid dullness; once more, we repeat, we should have neither positive expectations nor negative dreads.

There is a close connection between body and sensations; this is obvious because we feel every sensation somewhere in our body. The awareness on our body's breath—our awareness of our breath as the anchor previously described—comes from noticing or sensing the airflow while our breath is entering or leaving the nose. This airflow might be perceived at several adjacent places: in the nostrils, around the rings of the nostrils, below the entrance of the nose or on the upper lip.

The exact where's and how's of the above perception might be different for every person. Nevertheless, the consolidation of the first two foundations of mindfulness into one single item makes a very-easy-to-describe anchor out of the breath-sensations bond.[38] Meditators who choose to use this breath-sensations consolidated anchor may simultaneously observe the flow of air in and out of their nose and the subtle sensations, of whatever kind, that they perceive on and right above their upper lips. The meditators' attention is to be directed to the area at which the airflow *touches* the skin depending on where each individual feels the contact.

The Key Objective of Mindfulness Meditation

Summarizing the previous sections, mindfulness meditation, the starting point of the liberation from second arrows, is a sitting practice during which meditators, in a quiet environment, adopt a passive, purposeless, nonjudgmental attitude, and focus their attention on their breath or their body sensations.

Though we should approach mindfulness meditation with no gain or reward in mind, numerous benefits come from the practice of mindfulness meditation; they will be discussed later.

6. Mindfulness Meditation

For the time being, let us say that the main reason to meditate—in fact, the most important benefit of the exercise—is the development and growth of our ability to stay mindful—of our faculty of awareness—in our routine living. Meditation is about the learning and practice of attentiveness. When we are meditating, we are training our mind—more precisely, our brain—to be mindful.

Chapter 7 – Hindrances and Favoring Factors

Meditation Is Not the Goal

If meditation and mindfulness are so important—their practice brings about so many benefits that the academic world endorses both practices, health institutions recommend them, mass media discuss the subject frequently—and meditation leads to mindfulness, why do so few people meditate regularly?

Those reluctant to meditate commonly claim that its practice exceeds their capacity to focus attention and remain motionless for periods longer than a few seconds. This same kind of people, however, will seldom acknowledge that their mind is volatile and that they have difficulty to concentrate not only during meditation but also on their day-to-day tasks.

This deficit in concentration skills is what opens our mind to distractions and, more specifically, to cravings and aversions. The inability to meditate (what most everybody accepts) is not the problem; the real problem is the inability to focus attention (what very few people recognize). The more agitated our mind, the more we will benefit from meditation. Once again, we should practice meditation not to become good meditators but to be able to stay mindful for longer and longer periods.

Hindrances

What does prevent us from the practice of meditation and, consequently, from the habit of mindfulness? According to the Buddha, five hindrances,[39] or conditions—greed, hostility, sloth, restlessness and doubt—discourage us from practicing meditation or mindfulness; if we want to start either or both, we should manage such hindrances. Three of them—greed, hostility and restlessness—are very specific to the practice of meditation; the other two—sloth and doubt—

apply to the undertaking of any new endeavor. Let us review briefly these conditions.

Greed refers to cravings of all kinds, the acquisitive desires beyond reason for goods, food, sex, knowledge, prestige or power. Hostility includes all aversions—whether backed by reality or a product of fantasy—to people, things or events. As the mental formations they are, cravings and aversions are sometimes conscious—we are aware and tolerate our greed or hostility—or subconscious, manifesting as detrimental behavior or recurring digressions in our head.

Restlessness is the inability to focus our attention on anything. Restlessness originates in the permanent attacks of harmful cravings and aversions (that lead to greed and hostility) or harmless wanderings (that deviate attention).

Sloth is the continued failure to set sufficient time apart to meditate. This may be because we deny our anxiety-and-stress, we see it as no problem, or we place it low in the priority of our problems list. We usually do not set plans into action because we are too lazy to perform whatever tasks the new venture (for example, a new habit, hobby or project) demands.

Doubt is the lack of confidence in the positive outcome of meditation or the discounting of the practice as something ritualistic or fetishist. Doubt comes out of ignorance and is a close ally of sloth in our reluctance to initiate any kind of change.

Favoring Factors

Meditation and mindfulness become impossible without overcoming the five obstacles just described. What should students do? What circumstances or actions would remove or weaken these obstacles? The Buddha suggests seven favoring factors that help us to surmount the five hindrances; four are specific to meditation and mindfulness—attention to cravings and aversions, physical and mental calm, silence and equanimity—and three are of general application to any undertaking—determination, learning and joy.

The attention to cravings helps us to control greed; the attention to aversions does a similar job with hostility. Cravings and aversions, as mental formations, act from our subconscious mind; the very fact of paying attention to mental formations weakens them and facilitates our control.

Restlessness is the worst enemy of mindfulness; attention to cravings and aversions, physical and mental calm, silence and equanimity work in the management of restlessness.

We defeat sloth through determination, the fifth favoring factor; we must conquer sloth by pure power of will. Our acknowledgement of anxiety-and-stress—our acceptance of a real, conquerable problem—is the key ingredient in the stimulation of such determination. The more an illness hurts us, the harder we want to work on the healing therapy.

We overcome doubt through the certainty that results from learning; that is, from studying and understanding the problem and its solution. We should gain knowledge of how meditation works and we should learn from other people's experiences. The more we find out about the workings of anxiety-and-stress and the benefits of meditation, the more confident we will feel about undertaking its practice.

Beginners should look for information and guidance that help them to make up their mind; otherwise, they will get into a vicious circle: Their doubts will only vanish when they have directly experienced the benefits of mindfulness, and they will not start meditation until they are confident that it works.

Beginners should always undertake their mindfulness and meditation trip with joy—the seventh and last favoring factor—fully immersed in their resolution, with the enthusiasm of travelers going for the first time to places of well-recognized fame and beauty. Once at their destination, they will confirm the truth of what others told them; after that, their joy will be permanent.

Little by little, the practice of meditation, the continuous exercise of intensive focusing, will enhance mindfulness with a snowball effect, which will also become very helpful in the domination of the first three hindrances, that is, greed, hostility and restlessness.

Determination: The Key Favoring Factor

Some people, actually very few, find mindfulness as easy as if they were born with that attribute; for such people being attentive all the time seems to be the natural state of their mind. Many of those in this singular minority consider meditation an unnecessary exercise,[40] which demands substantial time off. Should these people ever decide to undertake meditation, its practice would come effortlessly.

Most of us, however, possess an agitated, digressing mind and have much difficulty keeping track of what is going on within our heads; the five hindrances to mindfulness do a good, pernicious job in disturbing our mind. This is why for us, the restless majority, meditation becomes a prerequisite for mindfulness and determination a prerequisite for meditation.

Out of the seven favoring factors, determination is the decisive one in our struggle against the difficulties of meditation. In fact, the continued application of this factor not only paves the way to our destination but also promotes and creates space for the activation of the other six favoring factors.

The easiest part of meditation is the set of instructions the new student is to follow. Any meditator with limited experience can easily describe such instructions for new students; newcomers do not require any previous knowledge or skill to begin the practice. From talk to walk, however, there is a long haul, and the actual practice of the *simple instructions* may become an arduous, tough endeavor for many people.

Meditating for ten minutes is a breeze; meditating for an hour is quite a different challenge.

Our determination pushes us to practice, practice, practice... repeatedly, persistently. We all know both from direct experience and from hearing it time and again, that practice makes mastery. We also know that the learning of complex tasks must begin with smaller, less complicated assignments—ball-juggling training begins with three balls. Therefore, when we start meditating, we know first, that we must persevere, and second, that we must focus attention on clear-cut anchors (such as our breath or distinct sensations).

Stories on how determination leads to fulfillment abound in all fields of human endeavors. Most everybody has witnessed or, at least, heard about such stories; sports chronicles of success through persistence are abundant and well documented. The following account illustrates the significance of resolve.

Alberto Sánchez, a high schoolmate of this author, was *determined* to become a successful goalkeeper from his early teen years; his training practices were indeed intensive. What a boring task! His coach threw him balls at close range, sometimes to the right, sometimes to the left. The practice went on for hours every day, for days every month. The prospective star had to catch as many balls as he could and he did so consistently. Long story short, as time went by, he became the goalkeeper for two well-known teams in his country and eventually for the Colombian national team.

Goalkeepers are trained with this routine (and many more) everywhere. Shuts are progressively harder and more difficult to catch and practices never stop. The goalkeepers' concentration on stopping every pitch, just grabbing the ball without thinking or evaluating, is equivalent to the meditators' focusing on each breath or each sensation, with no judgment or analysis. The application of mindfulness during our active hours and the ball stops in live matches are the actual situations during which meditators and goalkeepers, respectively, see the benefits of their training sessions.

Clearly, the continuous repetition of any task leads to its mastery; meditation does demand the determination successful sport players commonly display. While the aims and rewards of sports are mostly external—victory, recognition, endurance, money—and generally pursued, the compensations in meditation are inner and we should not run after them. In spite of the *required indifference* toward rewards, they do come: meditating becomes progressively easier and our day-to-day awareness skills, the *unsearched prize*, increase substantially.

What does the continuous repetition of a task, the outcome of determination in action, do to our brain? As neurologists know, our brain does change—stronger neuronal connections, more and longer branches in each neuron, even new neurons develop—when we reiterate over and over a task, be it ball catching, throwing balls at the basket, learning a new language or playing the violin. Something also happens in the brain of meditators. At some point, after persistent repetition, meditation becomes more simple and mindfulness more natural. Certainly, there are chemical and physical changes in our brain.[41]

What do those neuronal changes do to the practitioners of any repetitive task? Persistence pays and they become better skilled in performing the task, which therefore becomes easier. It is so for musicians, sport players, public speakers, cab drivers and, obviously, for meditators. The easing of meditation with intensive practice, however, seems to be faster than in other disciplines.

Mental Prayer

Mental prayer, an absorption practice of the Catholic Church, bears close similarities with the overall makeup of mindfulness meditation. This section presents such similarities and explains the rationale of making this comparison. Furthermore, some of the discrepancies between the two practices will also prove helpful to understand the importance of an unbiased mind while we meditate. Such discrepancies will be reviewed in Chapter 11 when the risks of some mental practices are discussed.

Mental prayer is a form of silent prayer practiced by the Catholic faithful whereby devotees concentrate their mind in the love of God and surrender their will to Him. Sixteenth century Catholic nun Saint Theresa of Jesus says that mental prayer is not an act of thinking much, but of loving much. (Paraphrasing Saint Theresa's statement, mindfulness meditation is not an act of thinking much, but of not thinking at all.) The expression *interior* prayer is often preferred instead of *mental* prayer to reflect the emphasis of the practice on emotion over thought—on heart over brain.

Other religions have equivalent rituals. For example, mental prayer and Sufism, the mystical dimension of Islam, are rather similar in their overall attitude toward their practices. Though Sufi meditational practices are very close to mental prayer, Sufi variations might include rituals such as recitation, singing and dancing. As expected, further differences come from the adherence of practitioners to the norms of their corresponding religions.

There is no method as such in mental prayer (or in Sufism). Two components seem to be fundamental: An absolute faith in God (or Allah) and in His mercy, and an unconditional acceptance of His will with a total detachment from worldly possessions or endeavors. Consequently, the person praying will humbly receive whatever God chooses to provide or decide, including poverty, sickness or even the disappearance of loved ones.

7. Hindrances and Favoring Factors

Meditation and Mental Prayer

Some people believe in the potential benefits of meditation (only partially covered so far) and, therefore, they would like to undertake its practice. Still the hindrances to their meditation seem to be doing their work and there is no sufficient determination to surmount them; in fewer words, they are not meditating.

Those people are far from alone in their frustration. The number of regular, everyday meditators, not only mindfulness but also meditation of all types, is extremely low compared with the billions of books and CDs that have been sold on the subject. The initial enthusiasm in meditation fades away rather quickly and only a fraction of the originally interested continues to practice regularly; most beginners quit meditation after a few weeks or months.

Is this negative trend going to change? There are some signs in that direction. Though the intellectual and academic interest on mindfulness is growing fast, the current base of committed students is still low. The total number of meditators, however, is not the important question for *me as the interested participant* and does not have any impact on *my* anxiety-and-stress. The key question is whether *I,* the person who would sit with eyes closed, should or should not meditate.

Each person must review his or her own suffering and take action accordingly. Other than recommending close attention to the hindrances and application of the favoring factors, there is only one further piece of information we would like to share at this point: The hardest part of the practice of meditation is the beginning; the difficulty of meditation decreases substantially as we gain experience.

Here is where the words of Saint Theresa of Jesus on mental prayer might prove encouraging; fortunately, the Catholic nun thoroughly documented her mystic experiences. [42] Though praying and meditating are quite different in purpose, they do have procedural resemblances. (Once more,

77

the similarities are in the processes of the two practices; their contents and goals are not only different but also conflicting.) The point to make—that the more often and longer we meditate, the easier the task will be—is backed by the beautiful metaphors with which the nun describes how effortless mental prayer will become when we apply sufficient patience and dedication.

Saint Theresa compares the decreasing difficulty of mental prayer with the methods countryside people in her time could use to irrigate their farms. Referring to prayer, she explains the easing sequence we can expect in the habit of meditation, leaving aside, of course, any religious context.

First and most burdensome, the Catholic nun thought the beginning of the practice (or meditation, in the comparison) is as taking water from a well to the farm, bucket by bucket, which requires, of course, huge, burdensome efforts. After a few days, things begin to improve with a second alternative, with which those devotees praying (or meditating) could use a treadmill to raise the water from the well and some channels to carry the liquid to their lands; this is still very difficult and onerous but it is less work and provides irrigation to the furrows.

With further persistence, a third choice becomes apparent; they could have irrigation ditches, which would carry water from a river or stream; the soil would get sufficient water, and farm owners would have to work much less. Nobody would have any complaint against starting mental prayer (or meditation) if it were this easy.

Finally, they could just adhere to the waters of the Lord (or the waters of a detached mind) and wait for His rains (its rains) to do the whole work; this would be the best option for the farmer and undoubtedly better than all the above. (This statement, which was probably accurate in the sixteenth century, might not hold true in the weather changing conditions of the contemporary world.)

"If you persevere in your contemplative prayers, God will not hide from anyone," said the Catholic saint. Rephrasing her words, if we persevere in our practice, mindfulness meditation (and mindfulness) will become easy and natural for us.

Through either the explanations of neurologists or the descriptions of mystics, however, we cannot persuade anyone about the easing evolution that follows the continuous practice of meditation. Only the direct experience of each individual will eventually erode his or her hesitation.

However difficult, if we are able to commit time to continued and frequent meditation sessions, we will become more and more aware of the multitude of events that our mind processes every minute during our daily lives and the way such events affect our behavior and our mental states. Then the ease, qualities and advantages of the challenging exercise will spontaneously show to practitioners.

Chapter 8 – Mental States

Meditation and Mental States

During meditation, we focus attention on specific anchors in order to enhance our mindfulness—to sharpen our faculty of awareness. Attention's anchors, as said earlier, come about in two categories: The first one comprises the anchors associated with the body and some of its functions; the second one covers the sensations throughout the body. Our breath is the king anchor in the body category; focusing on our sensations at one small body spot is the best example in the sensations category. The two categories connect each other intimately: when we direct attention to a part of our body, we *sense* it; we *feel* sensations throughout our body.

When we meditate, we train our mind to be passively attentive to our body and our sensations. Besides the passive awareness of our body and our sensations, mindfulness also demands the passive awareness of mental states. Can we—should we or do we need to—meditate using mental states as anchors?

While we could we sit in meditation and focus attention on the presence or absence of avarice, anger, partiality and so on, the observation of mental states refers mostly to the permanent *passive* awareness we should maintain of such states in our daily living. This means that, regardless of the actions we are performing at any time, we should stay attentive to *how our mind is doing.*

Yes, we could sit comfortably, in a quiet location, with our eyes closed, and mull over our mental states at every moment. No, we do not need to do so—in fact, this is not a desirable sitting practice—for a simple reason: It would be an unnecessary endeavor, and meditation instructions must be simple, within the ease of focusing attention on our breath and our sensations. Mental states are erratic and fuzzy, the kind of anchors not to use in meditation.

8. Mental States

Mind and Mental States

Returning then to mindfulness, how does our mind observe its mental states? More specifically, how does our mind observe what the same mind is doing? The examination of mental states is like *I* looking at *me*.

The roots of anxiety-and-stress—cravings, aversions and delusion—help us identify those harmful mental states to which we may be attentive. For example, avarice, attachment and jealousy are mental states connected to cravings; anger, hatred and disgust relate to aversions; partiality, fanaticism and chauvinism are associated with delusion.[43]

We do learn to stay passively attentive to mental states in our common activities through the continued practice of meditation with sharp attention on our body or our sensations. Mindfulness of mental states is similar to the impartial observation of our breath or our sensations; we simply notice the presence of avarice, anger, partiality or whatever, without judgment, without reaction, without trying to change anything. Appendix 2 contains the Buddha's guidelines for mindfulness of mental states.

We might sometimes become aware of body signals (our posture, our breath rhythm, our sensations) that come with the mental state of the moment; still we do nothing with whatever we come across. It is as if we were looking at our image in a mirror with no immediate possibility for modifying our race, sex, age or any other physical trait; we simply accept what is there. Neither should we expect anything to happen to us while we look at that image.

The beauty—and the trick—of mindfulness is that the observation of a mental state often deactivates the state. (No frustration is to arise if this does not happen.) This process is similar to what occurs in certain common situations; consider the following two examples. When somebody asks us why we are walking so fast, we most likely will slow down before answering; if the question is about what we are thinking, our mind might blank out for a moment, and we may need a few seconds to recall whatever our brain was doing.

The mental states we listed above, from avarice to chauvinism, are signs of anxiety-and-stress; they are harmful states and come from harmful mental formations. While we are mindful, it may happen that no harmful state is present or absent and, instead, we are going through some of the wholesome states that parallel inner harmony, such as detachment, tolerance, impartiality or fairness.

We should also become aware of these wholesome states, with no judgment, with no reaction, with no intention to modify anything. Wholesome states, as opposed to the harmful ones, do no deactivate when we observe them—they just stay there, and we are not to become proud or victorious because of these positive experiences. Sharp, impartial awareness of these mental states is as important as the observation of the harmful ones.

Sensations and Mental States

As said earlier, emotions and sensory signals occur mostly in our body (ex-brain)[44] while feelings and perceptions happen in our brain. The word *sensation,* one of the anchors of meditation, is used in reference to the combination of a sensory signal and its perception; though perceptions occur in the brain, we feel sensations wherever they happen in the body.

Suffering is a background feeling—blends of emotions, emotional recollections and sensory signals that produce the general tone of life. As we expand our faculty of awareness, we are increasingly mindful of sensory signals either associated with emotions (like racing heart, fast breathing or fist clenching), body conditions (like aches, motions or functions) or external contacts (like sights, sounds or touches). The result is improved awareness of both the background

8. Mental States

feelings and the full stream of changing feelings, or, in fewer words, improved awareness of our mental states.

We do not sit to meditate around mental states but, by focusing our attention on sensations while we meditate, we develop our faculty of awareness to become more mindful of the emotions and sensory signals that precede suffering.

Chapter 9 – Beyond Meditation

Eight Practices or Habits

Though meditation does have many benefits, its key purpose is the improvement of our faculty of awareness. Similarly, though mindfulness may bear some appealing advantages, its core objective is the freedom from suffering. Whatever the by-products of the exercises of meditation and mindfulness—health improvement, spiritual growth or emotions management, among many other—they should not distract us from the main intention, which at the very end is our liberation from anxiety-and-stress. Are there other things to do that push us in the right direction? Are there other procedures for the achievement of such a worthy goal?

Yes, some additional activities help us to stay on track as we struggle against cravings, aversions and delusion. No, they are not alternatives; they supplement and support the pursuing of the core objective. Mindfulness is the actual path toward the liberation from anxiety-and-stress and its practice, in and by itself, can lead to the desired destination.

Altogether, there are eight habits, or practices, that we should apply in our battle against suffering. These eight habits are views, thought, speech, action, livelihood, determination, mindfulness and mindfulness meditation. The adjective *mindful* is placed before the first five items, from views through livelihood, when referring to each of them by itself.[45] These eight practices are a combination of deeds and means that reinforce each other toward one-single goal; we can see them as both the approaches we take to fight suffering and the weapons we use in this peaceful combat.

Views and thoughts are grouped as the habits of wisdom; speech, action and livelihood are categorized as the practices of virtue; determination, mindfulness and mindfulness meditation come together as the practices of discipline.

The habits of discipline consist of active practices—they imply doing something. As explained next, the habits of wisdom (views and thought) and virtue (speech, action and livelihood) are passive—we have to restrain from doing certain things. The restraining from these *certain things* implies that we must be mindful of such things. In other words, mindfulness is on top of these five habits, therefore, instead of the words by themselves (view, thought, etc.), when presenting the habits in the following section, the adjective *mindful* precedes each habit (mindful views, mindful thought and so on).

Discipline

The review of the eight habits begins with the three practices of discipline. Though mindfulness and meditation have been discussed extensively, determination was briefly covered. Determination was first introduced as one of the mindfulness favoring factors—in fact, the key one. Determination leads to the overcoming of the barriers that makes us put off meditation and mindfulness.

By meditating and being mindful, we are effectively working on anxiety-and-stress. As we are able to develop our faculty of awareness, our journey toward the end of second arrows becomes progressively easier. The beginning of the path, however, might prove difficult and consequently our determination, as a habit, becomes critical. We should apply our determination not only to meditation and mindfulness but also to the two habits of wisdom and the three practices of virtue. Later on, *determination* will be further discussed, this time as the key agent of any personal or organizational transformation.

Determination as a Practice

As suggested earlier, suffering behaves like bacteria that are always ready to infest when we lower our guard. Our determination, our conscious exertion of willpower, should aim at controlling such bacteria by doing whatever favors our health and prevents us from getting sick. The measures to apply are actions such as staying away from places where bacteria are present, moving to locations where it is absent, vaccinating to prevent disease, taking antibiotics when we have already been infected, avoiding certain foods and so on.

Similarly, in our path toward the freedom from suffering, the habit of determination establishes four commonsense, self-evident recommendations.[46] According to these recommendations, we should:

1. Permanently reinforce and keep doing whatever is pushing us in the right direction.

2. Take whatever new actions will help us to accomplish our objective.

3. Stop doing anything that slows us down on our trip toward our anticipated goal.

4. Avoid doing those things that we are not doing now, but we know that, if performed, will damage us.

Accordingly, if meditating calms us down, let us meditate more; if being with some people distracts our mind away from problems, let us get together with those friends more often; if seeing sad movies depresses us, we should stop watching those movies; if somebody or something angers us, we should avoid such a person or event. In every case, we observe the feelings and thoughts entering our mind, and the sensory signals going through the body. We should not try to explain anything; just be aware of the experience.

The examples above make room for some rephrasing in the narrative of the habit of determination that switches emphasis from the activities as such—what we should do or avoid—onto how our mind feels and perceives such events. Consequently, to exercise the practice of determination, we should permanently be mindful of what every event does to our anxiety-and-stress: If an event decreases our suffering, we should duplicate the experience often; if it increases our anxiety-and-stress, we should avoid it.

Chapter 10 –Wisdom and Virtue

Passive Habits

Wisdom is the discernment and understanding of a mind that is free from cravings, aversions and biased opinions. The category of wisdom refers to the awareness of our inner world, to what is going on within our brain.

The two habits of wisdom—mindful views and mindful thought—are subjective; they happen exclusively within our brain and are invisible to others. The habits of views and thought do affect, however, the *visible* behavior of those cultivating them. Our views—impartial or biased—define the framework within which our thoughts develop. Thoughts, in turn, influence our speech, which affect our actions, which, in turn, have an impact on our livelihood. The whole chain is made out of strong links.

Virtue is the set of behaviors that favors the avoidance of second arrows and, consequentially, contributes to our inner harmony. The practices of virtue relate with the attention of our relationships with the outer world, more specifically, our interaction with other people.

The three habits of virtue—speech, action and livelihood—apply to our social behavior and are to be exercised in our daily interaction with the human groups that surround us. Unlike the practices of wisdom, which are private, the practices of virtue are public and manifest outwardly—they are readily noticeable.

With some differences in their applications or denominations, the habits of virtue appear in the precepts of most religions as well as in the codes of conduct of many groups and organizations.

The practices of virtue are plain common sense; the Golden Rule provides the best and shortest frame of reference for the meaning of virtue though it does not set precepts, commandments or codes of conduct. The words of Jesus in the Sermon of the Mount can hardly be more succinct or beautiful:[47] "Do to others whatever you would like them to do to you."

The Buddha's words that follow bear a similar meaning:[48] "As others are, so am I; as I am, so are others." In another text, the Sage says,[49] "See yourself in others; then who can you hurt? What harm can you do?" Though the wording in every religion might change, the essence is similar.

As the Golden Rule, the practices of wisdom and virtue, together with those of discipline, lead neither to rewards for good behavior nor to punishments for misconduct. Walking the path toward freedom from suffering does not take us to paradises; deviating from it does not place us in tormenting hells. There is no judge of any kind, up or out there, issuing a verdict or sanction at the end of the road; the judge is within us.

In the exercise of discipline, wisdom and virtue, the evil or good of anything we think, say or do—more accurately, its harm or benefit—comes from whether it increases or reduces our anxiety-and-stress. The punishment of our improper or harmful deeds is an intensification of our suffering, which eventually becomes intolerable; the reward for beneficial or wholesome acts is the progressive reduction of our suffering; when anxiety-and-stress finally ceases, the door to inner harmony widely opens. Either alternative—the penalty or the recompense—arises exclusively from our own behavior.

Mindful Views

Mindful views aim at impartiality. Views are the standpoint and way of looking at something—its parts, its qualities, the aspects we notice and so on. We commonly believe that the qualities of physical objects are self-contained and independent from the eyes of observers; nevertheless, the contents of an observer's mind interfere with whatever the reality out there might be. Every person sees each physical object differently. Sometimes the comments of several people about something are so different that we wonder whether everybody is looking at the same object.

When we consider subjective matters, such as stories, interpretations, theories, definitions or motives, views get bizarrely uncertain and dissimilar. Since such matters lack any kind of measurable reality, the experiences, feelings and predispositions of the judgers heavily color their view on the matter; at this point, such views become opinions.

Opinions are always biased; when they are on irrelevant matters, they cause no harm; there is no problem if we disagree on the quality of a movie or the reliability of an inoffensive story. However, as opinions enter social territories—religion, politics, race, affiliations to any sectarian cause, even adherence to sports teams—they become controversial beliefs that clash with other people's opinions and lead to discord and violence. Opinions become particularly relevant in metaphysical beliefs, the most abstract of all views, where the roots of all religions reside.

Addiction to opinions is a very subtle and common form of addiction. The workings of opinions are similar to those of cravings and aversions and, as said earlier, they cloud our understanding and lead to anxiety-and-stress.

People cannot throw away biased views easily because they are mental formations embedded as neuronal code in their brain. Our mind works with the images it develops of the outside world based on the sensory signals we receive through the senses; we always relate with those images through the associated mental formations, not with the objects they represent or the sensory signals our senses collect. We cannot interact directly with the inaccessible reality that is out there; we never know exactly how that *external* reality is.

For example, we hate or love the mental picture we have of a person, the mental formations that qualify the person for us, not the *reality* of that person—his or her actual physical and symbolic identities—because we will never know exactly what or how they are. If absolute realities were discernible, everybody would have exactly the same opinion of everyone else, and everybody would love or hate that individual, in exactly the same way. Consequently, hate or love for others comes from the mental formations of our opinions, which totally lack any observable physicality.

The proper attitude with respect to beliefs and biased opinions is impartiality. Impartiality, beyond fairness or rational objectivity, is detachment from opinions. "Right view is the absence of (biased) views," says Vietnamese Buddhist monk Thich Nhat Hanh.[50]

How do we detach from beliefs and biased opinions? How do we become impartial? The tactic is the habit of mindful views, that is, the application of mindfulness to our opinions; we have to observe them attentively and become aware of the feelings and perceptions that they generate in us. We cannot detach from something about which we deny our attachment.

When we are impartial, we have no affection for any opinion, let alone any interest in imposing our points of view on others. When we are impartial, our views are flexible and we can look at things from different angles. Impartial people also respect everybody else's beliefs. Impartiality disperses the clouds between the facts out there (the objects) and us (the subjects), and makes us truly neutral and conciliatory.

Mindful Thought

The appropriate application of the practice of thought, as a support to the elimination of anxiety-and-stress, is mindfulness of our thoughts. Generally, though not always, we are mindful of the thoughts that our brain *thinks* intentionally, as when we are working or writing.

Still, even when we are thinking on purpose, our brain is in permanent activity and generates digressions and distractions indiscriminately. Sometimes thoughts take our mind away from activities in which we need concentration (as reading or paying attention to someone talking to us); sometimes they run in parallel with those activities that do not demand full attention (as walking, driving or waiting for something).

How can we stay mindful of such random invasion? While mindful of our thoughts, we are not processing, judging or analyzing them; we are simply acknowledging their existence and their kind—thoughts of cravings as cravings, thoughts of aversions as aversions, thoughts of violence as violence. The intention of this practice is the absence of such thoughts.

Thoughts of violence are direct results from cravings, aversions and delusion (or biased views). When our craving demands are excessive or face competition for their fulfillment, our mind toys around with means for satisfaction, which easily lead to aggressive alternatives: I have to get this no matter how. Similarly, aversions in our mind may easily escalate to hatred, rage or other similar belligerent obsessions: This fellow will pay for that.

The righteousness that delusion engenders is an effective fertilizer of violence, both individual and social. When we hold biased opinions, we do not think by ourselves; our thoughts are framed by our biased opinions—our biases not only bring our mind to the biasing subject (for example, our ideology, our religion or our belief system) but also determine the way we are going to think. As we said before, because of the *certainty* of our religious or political opinions, we want to impose them on other people. The justification of our biased reasoning is straightforward: What is wrong with spreading the *truth*? If our opponents also possess their own truth, soon we will be facing a quarrel, if not an open conflict.

Most thoughts, fortunately, are inoffensive or neutral. They rotate around things we want—needs, appetites, pleasure—or things we do not want—threats, fears, pain. They can be about people who share our opinions and we love, or people who disagree with us and we hate. Desires for common needs and concerns about genuine threats are natural. Empathy with those who share our views and discrepancy with those who do not are also tolerable.

Cravings and aversions as well as sectarian zeal or hatred, on the other side, are different stories. In addition to being increasingly obsessive, cravings, aversions and biased opinions also embed the intention to act upon them—to obtain what we are yearning for, to avoid the objects of our loathing, and to enter into conflict for our biased opinions. Any element of this trio is definitely harmful and increases suffering. How do we manage it?

We cannot stop thoughts by power of will; we cannot follow the instruction *"Do not think of that person you hate."* Instead there are two alternative approaches that complement each other.

The first is the essence of mindfulness: We face our harmful thoughts; we focus our nonjudgmental attention on them, one by one; we do not elude or push away invasive thoughts, we confront them. This tactic slows down both the intensity and intentionality of the thought, which eventually fades away. This approach, a kind of open-eyes meditation, is useful when we are performing low-attention activities (like walking, eating or waiting in line).

The second is the anchors we use while meditating: We elude harmful thoughts; whenever we become aware of them, we switch our attention to any of the anchors we use in our practice of meditation: our breath (the most recommended), a particular sensation or a part of our body. While this approach is quite reliable when we are meditating, it may also prove effective in displacing the undesirable thoughts that come up and maintaining attention in the task we need or want to perform properly (like working on something, reading or playing chess).

The above recommendations are general guidelines. We have to remember that mindfulness is both active awareness of what we are doing (which pushes away unwanted thoughts) and passive awareness of body, sensations and mental states (which helps us to *detect* the unwanted thoughts when they arise).

Why is *thought* so important? Because thought precedes every mental state, so our thinking influences how we feel. Once more, the Buddha provides wise help to answer the question; he eloquently expands the previous sentence with metaphors:[51] "We become what we think. Suffering follows an evil thought as the wheels of a cart follow the oxen that draw it; joy follows a pure thought like a shadow that never leaves."

The Sage also provides another unselfish perspective: [52] "They abused me, mistreated me, defeated me, robbed me; harboring such thoughts keeps hatred alive. They abused me, mistreated me, defeated me, robbed me; releasing such thoughts banishes hatred for all time. For hatred can never put an end to hatred; only by non-hatred is hatred appeased." Evil thoughts and suffering go hand-in-hand; they are the fictitious second arrow of a real first arrow that did hit us in the past.

Similar advice applies to thoughts of greed, envy, pride, wrath or any other thoughts originating in cravings, aversions or biased views; those thoughts will always lead to anxiety-and-stress.

10. Wisdom and Virtue

Mindful Speech

Mindfulness of speech—the attention to the way we speak and the words we use—is a common instruction in every code of conduct and every handbook of good manners. Consequently, the practice of mindful speech is self-explanatory. A few things are noteworthy, however.

Mindfulness of speech is *easier* than mindfulness of thought. While we can think deliberately, our mind generates most of its thoughts involuntarily. Though sometimes our conversation might sound disorganized or confused, speaking is one activity that demands some level of orderly thinking. In fact, the more attentive we are to our thoughts, the less we have to apply attentiveness to speech; the habit of mindful thought filters much of what we speak.

Verbal speech is not the only language we use; human communications are also corporeal (postures, motions or gestures) and tonal (volume, inflection or emphasis) and our awareness should address these other expressions of language. Though written language lacks the corporeal and tonal components, we should also apply mindfulness to what we write.

The intention of exercising mindfulness on our speech is refraining from lies, malicious language, profanity and gossiping. Our awareness of everything we say (or write) is helpful in this direction. The Buddha is explicit in his recommendation:[53] "Never speak harsh words for they will rebound upon you." Next, the Sage explains why: "Angry words rebound and so does the hurt." Then we will suffer.

Mindful Action and Mindful Livelihood

Mindfulness of actions implies that we are permanently attentive of everything our body is doing. Though the previous sentence is comprehensive enough, the Buddha expands it in much detail to highlight certain actions that, in spite of their

being so natural or common, should be objects of our awareness. According to the Sage:[54]

> People who are mindful remain permanently conscious
> and fully aware of whatever their body is doing. Whether
> walking, standing, sitting, lying down or taking on any
> other stance, people who are mindful know precisely
> what their body is doing, and whatever posture it is
> adopting. Thus, in every situation, people who are mind-
> ful remain focused on their body just as a body.
>
> Whether they are going somewhere or coming back;
> whether they are looking straight or looking away;
> whether they are bending or stretching out; whether they
> wear light clothes or heavy clothes; when they are eating,
> drinking, chewing or tasting; when they are urinating or
> defecating; when they are walking, standing, sitting, fall-
> ing asleep, waking, speaking or keeping silent; people
> who are mindful know precisely what their body is do-
> ing. Thus, in every situation, people who are mindful re-
> main focused on their body just as a body.

As the habit of speech addresses the way we speak to other
people, the habit of action refers to the effect of our doings
on third parties. Specifically, the intention of the habit of action is our refraining from harming other people through violence, theft or sexual misconduct. Violence is the exertion of
force to injure a person; theft is the act of stealing; sexual
misconduct is having sexual encounters without the consent
of the partner or with partners who are already involved in a
relationship.

All the items that the Buddha details in the long quote above,
however, are motions or postures of the body and they do
not affect other people, except for matters of courtesy and
manners. How does this list connect with the intention of the
habit of action?

We use our body to do anything that has some visible goal or result—washing a car, placing our clothes in the closet, writing something, painting a wall, arranging objects on a shelf or whatever. We need to perform a number of subtasks to produce the desired goal or result. When we do such subtasks mindfully—with full awareness of our body, as the Buddha suggests—we also do them properly.

We also use our body when we hit someone, steal things or have nonconsensual or adulterous sex, and in these three situations we would perform certain subtasks to accomplish what we should otherwise refrain from doing. When we are mindful of both every subtask and the aim of the whole action, we are likely to reconsider everything and might abstain from carrying it through to its completion. We cannot be mindful and do harm to somebody simultaneously.

The practice of livelihood is the application of the practice of action—the refraining of violence, theft and sexual misconduct—to obtain the means of our subsistence. Our occupation should not: (1) encourage or deal with cruel or harmful behavior; (2) benefit from thieving, cheating or usury, or negotiate with stolen objects; (3) promote sexual commerce. In other words, our livelihood should exclude greed, hatred and lust.

Mindfulness and Determination

The sequence from views to livelihood, going through thought, speech and actions, is a tightly connected chain. The proper application of any practice influences the next one in the series, and so all the way down until the end of the chain. The result is a reduction of our anxiety-and-stress. Similarly, if we misuse any practice, the negative effect spreads down to the following links and necessarily our suffering will increase.

The positive, wholesome effect is evident. Mindfulness of our views strengthens mindfulness of our thoughts, which enhances mindfulness of our speech, and so on. The negative chain reaction with inattention is equivalent: Inattention to views leads to inattention to thoughts, to inattention to speech and so on.

We have been saying that, when we are mindful of any one of the habits in the chain, we apply the habit properly: In every case, we not only do the good thing but also we do things well. This translates into: (1) detached views; (2) thoughts free from cravings, aversions and violence; (3) speech free from lies, malicious language, profanity and gossiping; (4) actions free from violence, thefts and sexual misconducts; and (5) livelihood free from devious businesses.

Mindfulness and wrongness (biased views, violent thoughts, lies, thefts, etc.) are incompatible. We cannot do wrong (to others or to ourselves) when we are mindful of all the habits in the chain. Thieves might be very attentive of their actions while they sneak into their target destinations but they were not mindful of their selfish views and their thoughts while planning the robbery.

We have to remember that wholesome is what favors the elimination of anxiety-and-stress, and harmful is whatever produces suffering. In this sense, wholesome, right and good are synonymous words, and so are harmful, wrong and bad. In the context of Buddhist philosophy, however, these expressions are not in any way associated with morality, or with rewards or punishments arising from its correctness or incorrectness.

What if mindfulness is not enough, and we keep doing wrong and deviating from our path toward the cessation of suffering? The answer to this issue comes from the practice of determination. The application of determination takes place in two complementary halves: the exercising and reinforcing of whatever helps us in the elimination of second arrows, on one hand; and the avoidance or weakening of whatever moves us away from our goal, on the other.

Let us remember that the five practices from views to livelihood are passive habits, and that we apply them by refraining—by avoiding or weakening—from certain things, such as biased views, harmful thoughts, harmful speech, violent acts or incorrect trades.

If mindfulness is not enough for us to skip over all harmful views, thoughts, speech, actions and occupations, we must abstain from them, consciously and willfully. The avoidance and weakening of any harmful activity is the application of the second half of the practice of determination to our fight against anxiety-and-stress.

Can we actually liberate from suffering by the exclusive application of power of will? Can we control our cravings, aversions and biased opinions through the application of intention? We do not think so. Most views, thoughts, words and actions are governed by the neuronal code below our consciousness; so much so, that modern cognitive sciences are seriously questioning the actual level of human free will, if we have any at all.[55]

Determination does provide a certain degree of control over harmful formations; still we consider that this assistance, because it does not get to the root of the problem, is much more preventive than corrective. Some examples of precautions to take follow. If we are alcoholic, we should avoid taverns and drinking parties; if our weakness is lust, we should not watch porno movies; if we are the glutton type, we should not eat at buffet bars and all-you-can-eat places. Yes, there might be some people with such strong power of will that they have total control over all their doings, including views and thoughts; however, they are as uncommon, as the exceptional, born-mindful individuals.

The application of determination on the habits wisdom and virtue is indeed a weapon in our fight against anxiety-and-stress. Still the habit of mindfulness and the practice of med-

itation to develop our faculty of awareness is the safest path
to eliminate, or at least reduce, suffering.

Chapter 11 – Many Benefits and Some Risks

A Different Exercise

It has long been common knowledge that physical exercise grows and strengthens our muscular tissues. Likewise, though a more recent learning, it is also recognized that exercising our mind has a similar effect on our brain tissues. We train muscles by repeatedly tensing and loosening them; we train neurons by activating and deactivating them.

Mental exercise is the acquisition of new knowledge or the development of new skills. Both activities nurture the brain and both generate new neuronal connections; every time we learn something, additional neuronal links are established. The continuous exercise of physical and intellectual skills not only improves the utilization of existing neurons and re-develops deteriorating dendrites, the branches of neurons, but also favors the generation of some new nervous cells. In any of the three events—better use of existing capacity, longer dendrites or more neurons—there are more nervous connections and circuits to perform more tasks, in fewer words, more brain power within the same cranium.

At this point, some readers, particularly those who are more interested in meditation than in science, might be wondering why so much space is being dedicated to neurophysiology considering that the Buddha, the developer of mindfulness meditation, knew nothing about neurons or nervous systems. The reason for such coverage is easy to explain: Meditation is a mental exercise; its nature, however, is quite different from other brain training routines.

As said before, neuronal circuits communicate through elec-trochemical signals that influence the activity of neighboring target circuits. This influence is either excitatory—if it increases the activity of the target circuit—or inhibitory—if it decreases its activity. The training of the majority of excita-tory circuits that are undeveloped or inactive is the sphere of influence of both physical exercises (such as gymnastics or dance) and intellectual exercises (such as chess or cross-words).

The practice of mindfulness meditation operates mostly on inhibitory circuits. Just by sitting still, quiet, comfortable, with eyes closed and in an isolated place, a zillion excitatory connections go to rest (turn off) under the command of another zillion of inhibitory connections (that turn on).[56]

All this makes perfect sense. What do we do when we want to rest or sleep? We naturally follow similar steps—stillness, silence, comfort, closed eyes—and we might use some tricks, such as counting sheep or thinking about a beautiful sight, to induce somnolence. The benefits of sleeping seem to be primarily mental (as opposed to muscular, digestive, circulatory, or related to any other organ system) and its main beneficiary, the organ that needs it most, is the brain.

The difference between sleeping and meditation resides in the application that meditators make of mental anchors, the fourth element of the meditation guidelines; because of this difference, mindfulness meditation provides its practitioners with some mental benefits that the mere act of sleeping does not offer. The bodily and body functional mental anchors distinguish mindfulness meditation not only from sleep (where attention is off) but from other meditation techniques (which use *artificial* anchors).

Thanks to the selective functionality of our brain, we are not conscious of the large majority of the sensory signals occurring all the time in our daily life. With continued practice, meditators may exercise a certain degree of control over this functionality by favoring the spontaneous activation (turning on) and deactivation (turning off) of many sensory events, particularly of bodily sensations.

During meditation, we either stay focused on our anchor (hopefully most of the time) or are distracted. When we maintain focus on a particular item, we are inhibiting distractions, that is, we are holding thousands of inhibitory circuits on, and strengthening those circuits. As we digress, some inhibitory circuits turn off to allow the entrance of distractions. Consequently, inhibitory circuits iterate between on and off positions all the time. This continuous twinkling is what makes mindfulness meditation an intensive workout of our inhibitory mechanisms, a training of *passivity,* so to speak, and a very different kind of exercise. In Appendix 3, we explain the physiology of mindfulness meditation in much detail.

Benefits of Meditation

Living organisms always seek to maintain equilibrium; homeostasis is the biological self-regulation trait that restores such equilibrium when external conditions alter it. Thanks to homeostasis, our body, regardless of the outside conditions, maintains a constant temperature.

Stress is our bodily and mental reaction when external conditions disturb our balance and our homeostasis fails to restore it. Such failure occurs when either our body's internal corrective variables perform below healthy standards[57] or the magnitude of the disruption exceeds homeostasis's repairing capacity. This failure is bad for our body, our mind and our social interactions because it leads to all kind of disorders and diseases.

Mass media, both scientific and common, remind us constantly of the negative impact of stress on the quality of our lives. Those effects show up first in the body; they include a broad array of nuisances such as aches, weight gain or fatigue. Prolonged stress leads to chronic psychosomatic dysfunctions; the list includes digestive disorders (such as stomach ulcers), breathing problems (such as asthma), coronary diseases, rashes and migraines.

Stress does not only attack the body; it also hits our mental and social lives. In the territory of moods and feelings, stress effects show up with many faces—depression, restlessness, sadness, etc. As if this was not enough, sooner than later, stress takes its toll on our behavior, where it may lead to alcohol or drug abuse, changes in appetite or sleep patterns, reduced sex drive or social withdrawal.

Still these are not the only impacted areas. Stress also disturbs our immune system, and makes us easier victims of infectious diseases (viral, bacterial or parasitic), because of the decline of our body's defenses.

There are many stress management strategies; they may be physical exercises, cognitive approaches, relaxation methods or combinations of these three approaches. In the ranking of effectiveness of the large number of stress management therapies, meditation, in general, and mindfulness meditation, in particular, are in the upper places of the list.

The immediate benefit of meditation techniques in general— mindfulness, yoga, zazen, transcendental, etc.—is the solution or reduction of the problems stress creates. Meditation does alleviate everything stress damages but it does not make us eternal. Aging, lifestyle or heredity will eventually bring many of us to some painful degenerative diseases, such as cancer or arthritis. Meditation is also helpful in these misfortunes because it not only makes us less prone to these diseases but also, if they get us, we will suffer less.

The practice of meditation significantly increases our pain threshold and our capacity to cope with adversity (a similar effect occurs in people with deep religious devotion). The result is that, when attacked by those horrendous maladies otherwise unbearable, meditators become more tolerant to pain; for them, such woes really ache less and inflict less emotional damage on them.

11. Many Benefits and Some Risks

There is not much need to spend more space on the subject of general benefits. Since the damages of stress in all aspects of our life—physical, psychological and behavioral—are so devastating, their control and amelioration by meditation does not need much advertising.

In summary, stress impairs our body's health and undermines the overall quality of our life. Physical pain closely follows stress; it is safe to say that the pain that does not come from external agents (accidents, blows, knives…) is a kind of *thermometer* that gauges the *fever* of stress, and meditation is like an aspirin that helps with every stress problem.

The expression *anxiety-and-stress* is not used in this section; the word *stress* by itself is preferred on purpose. Everybody is familiar with (if not tortured by) stress. The academic world has done much research on stress—not on anxiety-and-stress,[58] the synonym used for suffering.

Benefits of Mindfulness Meditation

In the health area, mindfulness meditation delivers the same level and kind of stress-related benefits as other sitting meditation techniques; such benefits provide in and by themselves enough incentives to undertake its practice. There is more for mindfulness meditation, however; its specific advantages reside in the strengthening of inhibitory circuits, and in the increase of our ability to stay mindful throughout our regular hours.

The first advantage, the strengthening of inhibitory circuits, is a corollary of the intensive work out that the nervous system inhibitory mechanisms undergo during the practice of mindfulness meditation. The inhibitory capacity of our nervous system deteriorates because of underuse or misuse. This is why we keep eating when we are already full, and we fear imaginary threats or past setbacks that are under control now. Mindfulness meditation brings inhibitory circuits back to order.[59]

The second benefit, the increase of our ability to stay mindful, is precisely the skill we train when we meditate. Our mind wanders a lot and meditation is about making it wander less. On average, according to studies on the subject,[60] we are distracted from the task of the moment, the one that is keeping us busy, around forty percent of the time.

While meditating or otherwise, digressive thoughts come uncalled all the time, and they *attack* relentlessly with the ammunition they get from the whole deposit of our memories and mental formations. While meditating, either we are focused (we are keeping the intruders away) or we are digressing (the intruders are hitting the target). When this happen, we go to breathing attention for help, and we regain focus.

We have to do this many, many times. Even if meditation is not the inhibitory circuits' strengthening exercise that we trust it is, the recurrent practice of any activity, physical or intellectual, makes us better at its execution. Continuous repetition of meditation sessions leads to right practicing (much focusing, little digressing); repetition of the right practice leads to mastery (minimum digressing); mastery of mindfulness meditation leads to increased mindfulness during our alert hours (an attentive mind most of the time).

Benefits of Mindfulness

Most distracting thoughts—the person we met yesterday, the book we are reading, the appointment we have next week—are inoffensive and, up to a certain extent, useful—we do need to remember the name of that person, we do not want to forget the plot of the book, we must not miss that appointment.

A certain degree of wandering is not only harmless but it may prove useful; when we are distracted, some experts in creativity claim, we may inadvertently resolve some problems that have broken our heads for days. The real troubles begin when we start wandering around our harmful formations—our cravings, our aversions and our biased opinions.

Innocuous ideas come and go; we just jump from one thought to the next in an almost random sequence. Cravings and aversions, however, are persistent and stay in the vanguard of our thoughts' thread; this is so because they are distortions of appetites and fears, respectively, and behave as such. Appetites and fears are survival traits; for our organism, whatever it interprets as survival—appetites, fears or their distortions—means highest priority.

Biased opinions—our fanatic beliefs on political systems, religious dogmas, sports team affiliations, etc.—also rank high in the digressing game. Our mind wanders enthusiastically around our idols, which lead or share our fervors, and grumbles angrily about the signs and symbolic characters of what we hate.

Our trend to engage in sectarian or doctrinarian affiliations is a distortion of our normal sense of belonging, the inborn predisposition to be part of some group or organization. A number of scholars consider the sense of belonging[61] as a basic need of human nature; we could arguably say that, as appetites and fears, this attribute is also a survival trait.[62] Since lonely specimens, now and one million years ago, leave fewer children, our ancestors were, thousands of generations ago, the companionship seekers. In other words, natural selection favors the social ones; the lonely ones tend to die with no children and, well, alone.

However we have developed them, cravings, aversions and biased opinions, harm us and are the roots of suffering; mindfulness keeps them at bay and, in the process, it frees us from anxiety-and-stress. This is the core benefit—the beauty, the incentive, the reason—of mindfulness. There cannot be too much emphasis on this fact. Consequently, the repetition of the words of the Buddha that were quoted earlier is appropriate:[63] "Mindfulness is the only path for the overcoming of anxiety-and-stress, for the cessation of suffering, for the attainment of inner harmony."

How does mindfulness help us to handle cravings, aversions and biased opinions? In other words, how does mindfulness liberate us from suffering? Though the question is unambiguous and direct, the answer requires some clarification. Our brain registers those events that eventually become mental formations, and embeds their code in the neuronal program of our self. Since this is a dynamic program, its size and complexity change as mental formations come and go.

Regardless how many or how few mental formations we have developed and coded in our brain through time, the neuronal program of every moment—the ruling self of the minute—manages us. The neuronal program of our self controls the totality of our doings—the views we hold, the thoughts we wonder about, the words we pronounce, the actions we take, and the works we do to make our living. This is a truly interconnected chain; these five links together might not always mediate in all our doings but there is much interaction between them.

By being mindful of the whole chain, we are aware of and have *spontaneous power* over each link: biased opinions as the frames of wandering thoughts, thoughts about what we are going to say, words that may anticipate what we are going to do, and actions that contribute to our livelihood. On top of that, we also are to be mindful of our body, our sensations (the perceptions of sensory signals), and our mental states.

This simultaneously piecemeal and total awareness—the awareness of each item individually and of the whole set—slows down the automatic, uncontrolled reactions of mental formations and eventually stills them. Little by little, the essential self, the subject of the next chapter, takes over. This essential self brings about a behavior that it is spontaneous and does not have the contamination of harmful mental formations.

The power that mindfulness puts up in our brain is the capacity to act in every circumstance without the manipulation of negative mental formations, as if their records did not exist in our brain. For example, if we meet with somebody we hate, a hate-that-person mental formation somewhere in our frontal cortex activates. If at that very moment, we become aware of our hatred, we should be able to bypass the mental formation and see him or her as we did originally, before his or her offensive action had occurred. As this happens, our hatred toward this individual softens and eventually vanishes.

When we mindfully observe a craving, an aversion or a biased view, *ready to attack* and prompt some unwanted behavior on us, our mindfulness *denounces* such a craving, aversion or bias view, *before* they make decisions for us. Then we put mental formations on hold and act freely as if those mental formations did not exist. Although we still might end up doing something in the direction the associated mental formation was triggering, when we act mindfully, the actions will be conscious as opposed to uncontrolled. For example, when we unexpectedly come across a person we dislike, we mindfully and consciously might greet him or her just indifferently while the associated mental formation, out of animosity, might be demanding verbal aggression.

A metaphor should help. The process of our inner mindfulness is similar to the third-party *mindfulness of friends or family* when at a social gathering they make a drunken person realize—they make that individual mindful—that he or she has had too much to drink. (Yes, such acknowledgement does not come easy; the application of our own mindfulness, even when we are not drunk, is not easy either.)

If this individual, in spite of the intoxication, admits such condition, there occurs a pause of awareness in his behavior that changes everything: The person stops drinking alcohol at that moment, might instead ask for some water, will accept his or her inability to drive, will express consideration to whomever he or she has mistreated, might sleep for a while... Mental formations, as the alcohol of the story, are similar to drugs in that they alter what otherwise would be straight conduct.

Mindfulness of mental formations—always ready to attack— is mindfulness of the suffering they are generating. The more intense our perceptions (of the involved sensory signals) and feelings (of the involved emotions) behind cravings, aversions or biased views, the more apparent anxiety-and-stress is.

A couple of examples of each one of the three harmful mental formations should help our understanding. Greed and lust are expressions of cravings; hatred and anger, of aversions; and racism and fanaticism, of biased opinions. All of them manifest throughout our body in different ways and become combinations of feelings and perceptions when our brain registers what is going on in our stomach, muscles, heart, mouth, or wherever they are showing up.

When we carefully observe the perceptions and feelings that those mental formations produce, we might choose to ignore the source (whatever is producing our greed, our lust, our hatred...), and maintain awareness of the results (the perceptions and feelings) and *keep walking*. For example, when somebody calls us names, as we hear the physical noise of the insult, we also feel our muscular tension increasing and our fists clenching; thanks to mindfulness, our body signals channel our attention and we are able ignore the provoker.

Alternatively, we might shut our mindfulness off and disregard perceptions and feelings as well as mental formations, altogether, as if they did not exist. When we do this consistently, the doings and effects of mental formations blend with our daily behavior, and we become permanently greedy, lustful, rancorous, angry, racist or radical extremist individuals. "That is how we are!" we might say. In the worst cases, we even express amusement for such abnormal traits and brag about them. This is suffering biting us, no matter how much we ignore or deny it—we do not know or we do not want to know that it is there.

Does mindfulness erase the neuronal code of harmful formations? That does not seem to be so; they probably sit dormant somewhere in the frontal cortex and any relapse will revive the original craving, aversion or biased view. (Stories of how the flame of passion reignites in former lovers in their first encounter after decades apart abound. Yes, romantic love is a mental formation that may be fulfilling and wholesome, or frustrating and harmful.)

Mindfulness and mindfulness meditation are intimately connected and support each other in a virtuous circle: If we meditate, we can stay mindful longer, which makes meditation easier, and so on.

The following sequence summarizes the whole process from meditation (the starting point) to inner harmony (the outcome): (1) mindfulness meditation strengthens inhibitory neuronal circuits; (2) which increases our ability to stay mindful; (3) which keeps cravings, aversions and biased views at bay; (4) which puts the neuronal code of harmful mental formations to sleep; (5) which eliminates or reduces suffering; (6) which opens the door to inner harmony.

To close this section, the benefits of mindfulness and mindfulness meditation are recapitulated in an upward progression. The following series presents such benefits as they might manifest in the lives of people walking their paths toward the end of suffering. The twin habits of mindfulness and mindfulness meditation:

1. Reduce stress.

2. Resolve stress related disorders, be they physical, emotional or social.

3. Strengthen our immune system.

4. Increase our pain threshold.

5. Strengthen our inhibitory neuronal circuits.

6. Help us manage and control cravings, aversions and biased opinions.

7. Eliminate or reduce suffering.

Are Mindfulness and Meditation Natural?

We humans possess scores of traits and faculties. Some, such as eating or mating, we share with other living beings; others, such as thinking or speaking, are exclusive to us; all are inherent to us, that is, they are natural—they are part of our biological design.

Is mindfulness natural? Are we born with this characteristic and we lost it—some animals seem to be permanently attentive—or is it something we have to develop? Though there do not seem to be definitive answers to these questions, most everyone agrees that the exercise of mindfulness is a difficult task to perform, which raises doubts about its *naturalness*— its innate quality.

It is easy to speculate, though, that the brainwork involved in mindfulness is quite similar to the sharp attention that wilderness living should have imposed on our distant ancestors. Long before becoming themselves carnivorous and predators, our forebears were non-carnivorous vegetarians and easy prey for aggressive animals. Only those individuals who were attentive all the time to both the sensory signals in the environment—sounds, forms, smells—and the careful motions of their body, were able to anticipate killers, move silently and so survive enough to leave offspring.

11. Many Benefits and Some Risks

Considering that natural selection might have led us to some predisposition toward mindfulness is not a farfetched hypothesis. If so, our brains might have a natural inclination to focus attention that we do not always develop. It is also evident that, during the millennia that preceded the discovery of fire and the development of language, our prehistoric ancestors, with an elementary brain that hardly thought, had to adjust to stay awake, in darkness, still and quiet, both body and mind, for millions of long nights.

It is probably too bold to suggest that mindfulness and mindfulness meditation are characteristics implanted in our nature. On the other extreme, it would be too timid to say that these two habits are genetically foreign to us, modern humans. Still it is safe to state that something in our body and our brain is there to facilitate meditation and mindfulness.

Meditation, in general, is neither more nor less natural than aerobics or sports. Our distant precursors ran a lot and did not ponder much; they went everywhere on foot, and lacked any kind of relaxing furniture on which to sit or rest; they indeed struggled for their livelihood in open spaces, and lacked safe, fixed workplaces.

Very slowly for many millennia and suddenly high-speed over the last decades, humankind progressed extraordinarily and machines took over most of our hard work. Thereafter modern humans stilled their body—they remain sitting most of the time in comfortable chairs or couches—and disturbed their mind—they hardly stop thinking, digressing or worrying.

In reaction to their immobility, *Homo sapiens* invented all kinds of calisthenics—rather recently, we should say; to counter mental agitation, the humans of the third millennium are recapturing the old tradition of mindfulness meditation, a tool to appease their restless mind.

Risks of Mindfulness Meditation

The risks of meditation are not unique or exclusive to the practice itself; its hazards are common to almost any altered state of consciousness, the wide range of mental states that deviate from normal waking conditions. [64] Drug-induced states, runners' highs, sleep dreaming, mystical raptures and, of course, deep meditative states are examples of altered states of consciousness.

People going through altered states of consciousness become extremely vulnerable. The neuronal commotion of the phenomenon results in a sort of mental anarchy during which the participants' beliefs—their biased opinions—may drastically affect their senses and, consequentially, their interpretation of reality. If some agent (teacher, tutor, therapist, healer, charlatan...) facilitates or induces such states, the subject of the experience may surrender his or her willpower, and the agent may take it over.

During an altered state of consciousness, as in sleep dreaming, people might see, hear, touch or smell things that do not exist or experience events that are not happening. There is no problem with this, except when subjects take such fictions as real.

Trances, ecstasies and raptures—three words with close connotations—are specific cases of altered states. According to some subjects, people under these conditions may also go through some pleasant perceptions which they describe in abstract terms such as timelessness, cosmic unity, extinction of identity, a different reality or disappearance of body boundaries. Though it is not possible to qualify in intensity, or quantify in duration or frequency, these episodes are liable to occur during deep meditation. Some individuals seem to be more predisposed and sensitive to these types of experiences than the average person is; however, there is no research work, that this author knows, that supports such a statement.

The influence of meditators' belief systems and the intervention of dishonest agents are two interconnected aspects that are detrimental to the equanimity we should maintain during meditation. In the following paragraphs, we want to describe the way mindfulness meditation handles such risks.

During induced or pursued altered states of any kind, the subjects' biased opinions (those that are embedded in their belief system) have a determining effect on the illusory perceptions subjects create; all the metaphysical beings of their doctrine and cult—gods, angels, saints and, yes, demons in satanic rituals—might become visible and audible in the fabricated reality. Whatever happens during the experience transforms then in a *revealed* truth, an unquestionable manifestation of some higher-dimension entity.

Deep faith, intense religious zeal and mystical trances become a self-reinforcing circle: Mystical trances strengthen faith, which incites further religious zeal, which leads to more intense mystical experiences and so on. Mysticism is common to all religions; mystics from all creeds do go through paranormal experiences that are beyond down-to-earth analysis and common logic. Every mystic interprets the phenomena of his or her ecstasies as direct interventions of their corresponding divinities.

Indian philosopher J. Krishnamurti, a non-affiliated twentieth century thinker, is one exception to the commonly accommodated metaphysical explanations of mystical experiences. Based on the sharp, non-biased observation of his multiple encounters with altered states, during which he could see and speak with apparitions of *spiritual masters,* the philosopher concludes that the human intellect projects its contents into the sensory experience. When this happens, some people, in the anarchy of altered states, may end up seeing and hearing what they unconsciously want to see and hear.

During a public talk, while answering a question about the masters of the Theosophical Society,[65] Krishnamurti said,[66] "When I was a small boy I used to see Sri Krishna,[67] with the flute, as he is pictured by the Hindus, because my mother was a devotee of Sri Krishna... When I grew older and met the Theosophical Society, I began to see their spiritual masters in the form they were put before me and they were the ultimate end. Later on, I began to see the Lord Maitreya...[68] Now lately, it has been the Buddha whom I have been seeing, and it has been my delight and my glory to be with him."

When the Indian philosopher left behind all religious doctrines, he stopped undergoing such mystical trances, or they evolved into something of a different, neutral nature. After this transformation, Krishnamurti never spoke again about his mystical encounters.

Deep meditation, as already said, is also an altered state of consciousness, during which some people might reach ecstatic experiences. The main reason to quote Krishnamurti's words is to emphasize the importance of neutrality when we undertake meditation. If we hold any kind of biased view— for example, deep well-intentioned religious faith or bigoted, prejudiced, sectarian opinions—at the start of a meditation session and we refuse to acknowledge such opinions as unnecessary discretionary mental formations, our subjective beliefs might take over our mind and distort our experience. Our delusion, that we expected to remove through meditation, might become murkier than when we started the practice. In summary, we will become *more* prone to suffering, not less, as we would have wanted.

When, on top of our biased mind, dishonest agents enter the scene, things worsen even further. These kinds of individuals assume authority over their subjects' will and may manipulate them in wicked ways—financially, behaviorally, sexually, etc. Moreover, such crooked agents will do their best to enslave their subjects and block any possible avenue toward liberation.

Regardless the technique, meditation guidelines should thwart the hideous scenarios of biased views and dishonest intermediaries. Mindfulness meditation controls both risks from their roots and aims at the avoidance of such an undesirable state of affairs.

In mindfulness meditation, there are not—there must not be—authoritarian figures behind the practice—no master, swami, guru or spiritual guide—beyond some non-sectarian instructor who describes for us the simple steps we should follow. Though written or recorded directions are enough for many people to start the practice, the guidance of a trustworthy teacher may prove useful, particularly during the early sessions, until the new student flies solo. This specific point will be expanded later.

This book's recommendations as to where to focus attention during meditation, namely, on our body and our sensations, promote neutrality. There is no room for biases or judgments around such instructions. Images, symbols, chants or mantras as meditation anchors, on the other hand, are incompatible with the short list of mindfulness meditation guidelines. With the use of such non-natural—non-physiological—devices as anchors, meditators run the risk of developing attachment to those devices, or devotion to the teacher who promotes them, and elaborate *fictitious realities* build around the artificial anchors' projections in the practitioner's mind.

We also have to bear in mind the nonjudgmental and non-religious character of mindfulness meditation. When we are mindful, during meditation or otherwise, we should not assess or try to explain the events that are going through our whole body—our sensory machinery, including our brain. We should only observe things as they come and go, and leave aside any intention to interpret what is happening.

The only purpose of mindfulness meditation is to improve our ability to be mindful; the only purpose of mindfulness is the reduction and eventual elimination of anxiety-and-stress. We should not assign, by any means, any religious content or context to mindfulness meditation; there are no beliefs of any kind behind it, much less beliefs in immaterial entities or metaphysical events; there are no rituals to follow for any purpose or reverences to pay to any being. This neutrality sets apart mindfulness meditation from prayer, in general, and Saint Theresa's mental prayer, in particular.[69]

The fact that we should disconnect beliefs and rituals from mindfulness meditation does not mean that we have to abandon our religion, deny its doctrine, stop going to churches or temples, or ban religious ceremonies before starting meditation or during our continued practices. Meditators just need to place mindfulness and mindfulness meditation on one side, and dogmas and cult on the other; they are two different avenues, with different destinations.

After practicing mindfulness meditation for a while—the length of this *while* changes a lot from person to person—we will start looking at our belief system from a different perspective. The perspective that each individual develops is personal; mindfulness meditation intends neither to change the beliefs of the practitioner nor to seed new ones in their mind. Certainly, though, the perspective toward which we evolve after meditating for some time, continuously and persistently, will be one of impartiality and tolerance.

Chapter 12 – Essential Self

The Size of the Self

As a brief introduction to this chapter and an aid to its proper understanding, it is convenient to go over the notions of self and redundant ego that were covered earlier. The self rules are coded in our brain; they consist of both data and software. The data is everything we know or can do, and everybody we can name or relate to, that is, all our wholesome and harmful mental formations. The software is the instructions for doing things with the data. These instructions manage our behavior. When we need to add seven plus nine (the data), the addition rules in our head (or how we should use our fingers) are the instructions; when we see somebody we like (the person's face matches a piece of data), then we should look happy ("smile!" is the instruction).

Redundant ego is the portion of the self that grows out from cravings, aversions and biased views—the harmful mental formations: the desire for that food we should not eat, the hatred to that person who failed us, the unconditional support to our political party.

Everybody agrees that we have a sense of identity; we feel it—*I know I exist because I think and I sense a body that I consider mine.* It is harder to accept, however, that the share of the self that results from our harmful mental formation is superfluous or optional. We refer to this extra chunk of self as redundant ego. Because of this redundant ego, that may be small or large, we can say that the self has a sort of variable size.

Why do we talk about *a sort of* variable size? Saying that the self has a certain size does not mean we can measure it. We cannot quantify the magnitude of the self—anybody's or ours—because such magnitude is, besides variable, diffuse and intangible. The self is a combination of data and software in the brain, and it does not have borders, frames of reference, mass or volume that we can gauge or weigh.

The self is also invisible; we can only sense its manifestations through the actions it programs and our body executes. In other words, we do not have access to the neuronal data or code that builds the self (as we never touch the instructions of the operating system in our personal computer) but we discern—see, hear, sense—physical actions, emotional behaviors and mental expressions (as we can look and analyze the output of the computer programs we use). The clearest expression of *my* self's software is the specific differentiation it makes of who I am (versus the others), and what it defines as mine (versus somebody else's).

Dimensioning our self is as impossible as measuring any other phenomena of the mind, such as dreaming, feeling, loving, thinking... We may talk about a vivid dream or an intense feeling but we can only speculate that more vividness or more intensity merely means that there are more neuronal circuits involved in the dream or the feeling. That is all.

Though neurologists and psychologists would love to estimate the size of the self (the latter by looking at the areas of the brain where the self manifests; the former, through personality tests), this characteristic is not *sizable*. However, an attribute that starts near zero in a newborn, increases slowly with the child's chronological age, adjusts in different ways during adolescence, somewhat stabilizes in adulthood and goes back to minimum as we approach death, must have, however diffuse, a certain magnitude.

Does it make any sense to speak about the size of such an abstract term as self? Though winds are well-understood physical phenomena, they have some similarities with the notion of self. The self is neuronal instructions in action; winds are streams of air in motion. A self and a wind both have diffuse sizes, still both also have intensities and territories. We can measure a wind's speed and determine the areas where it is blowing; though we cannot calculate it, we can *sense* the intensity of some selves (of some symbolic identities) and the ways they are manifesting. Within the freedom they offer, we close this metaphor saying that, when we reduce the size of our self (as we are going to discuss next), we are slowing down the mental wind and reducing the region where it is gusting.

Trimming Redundancy

We know now that the undefined size of the self does change sharply—up from birth to adolescence and down from old age to death; it changes as we go to sleep, we drink alcohol or use drugs. We can also say that there are size variations when we develop a new habit, take ownership of some good, fall in love or start hating something or somebody. In a broader sense, our self's size increases every time we add mental formations or data of any kind in our neuronal database.

Beyond the specific situations we described above or the additional ones that we could think of, can we willingly influence our *overall* self's size? The answer is affirmative; yes, we can influence the magnitude of the vast web of the neuronal circuits that generate our sense of identity, as well as the intensity of the corresponding expressions of our individuality associated with those circuits. Definitely, we can have some bearing on this important matter and we do it more often than we might think.

The upward expansion occurs spontaneously, through new, involuntary attachments, which generate additional neuronal circuits or strengthen the existing ones; we *normally* want more money, prestige, friends or the like. By opening ourselves to these licenses we are letting air into, when not blowing in, our self's globe. This is to say that we are willingly favoring the growth of our self.

Downward, the contraction of the self occurs when we detach from our cravings, aversions and biased opinions. We can accomplish this, the hard next-to-impossible way, through harsh self-control and earnest renunciation to whatever enslaves us. Alternatively, we can do the same—it also demands determination—through the practice of mindfulness meditation.

When we succeed in either case, detachment results from the activation of lots of inhibitory circuits, which, in turn, weakens or switches off similar numbers of neuronal excitatory circuits—the ones that make us demand more food, wealth, fame or social interactions.

Growing selves (growing redundant egos) are very apparent. As we keep adding all types of possessions—material, intellectual, emotional, etc.—or, better said, as we become attached to such things, our self inflates and toughens. Although we distinguish other people's large redundant egos, we commonly do not notice the expansion of our self—too bad for us; our self is unable to assess its own load.

At the other end, we often overlook the humility of detached and benevolent people, whose small-sized selves lack presumptions of any kind. Selfless individuals, unsurprisingly, are unaware of this virtue—any presumption of their humility would make them arrogant; they seldom voice opinions about others.[70]

Mindfulness meditation is the trustworthy tool to downsize our self. Since meditation is a practice we voluntarily undertake, such downsizing is deliberate—it is something we do on purpose: We turn on the trimming machine for as long as we want but the machine does the work by itself; mindfulness meditation is an easier, more reliable approach than renunciation.

How does the downsizing of the self happen? Mindfulness meditation retrains our inhibitory mechanisms to perform their jobs—the duties they have forgotten—that is, the halt of appetites for artificial needs, of fears to imaginary threats, and of attachments to groundless views. Moreover, as already said several times, meditation trains us to be mindful (of body, sensations and mental events) and mindfulness dutifully reinforces our ability to control cravings, aversions and biased views in real time. The control of this fatidic trio is the right way to manage the size of the self.

Harmful mental formations make up the redundant ego. Redundant ego is that unnecessary, artificially increased portion of our self that we can and will suppress when we undertake the exercise of mindfulness.

How does mindfulness meditation suppress the redundant ego? We could think that our redundant ego is like a number of neuronal routines for every mental formation that contain both the data about the events that prompt them (the stimuli) and the instructions for what is to be done next (the responses).

We have to remember that mental formations are distortions of inborn mechanisms. While it is natural to want something to eat when we are hungry, it is abnormal to desire food, as happens to bulimics, when we are full; this is a harmful formation. The stimulus to this mental formation might be seeing, smelling, thinking or talking about foodstuff; response is the instruction to eat something right away.

Mindfulness meditation does not erase or change *natural* neuronal routines and does not make anorexics out of bulimics. To survive, we must keep our desire for food and our intention to eat when we are suitably hungry. What mindfulness meditation actually does is retrain our inhibitory circuits to keep us off the spoon once we are full.

Our suffering is in direct proportion to the *size* of our redundant ego. The suppression of the redundant ego—this is what happens during downsizing—results from the reactivation of myriad inhibitory circuits that were not doing their jobs.

From then on, the retrained circuits will deter us from over-eating, drinking too much, yearning for the unnecessary, hating for no reason, getting mad for silly things, frightening for nothing, prejudging... Then anxiety-and-stress ends.

Downsized Self

The self is the supreme arrangement of our brain and one of the outstanding characteristics of human nature. No other species on Earth displays such an attribute—definitely not in the degree of perfection that human beings exhibit it. The self is the unequivocal identity—our symbolic identity—that expresses when we say *I, me, mine, myself*; sets boundaries that define *here* from *there* and *this* from *that*; and differentiates between *me* on one side, and *you, him, her or them* on the other.

With some exceptions originating from uncommon neurological anomalies, all humans display their first hints of individuality soon after birth. The trait of the humans' symbolic identity is the summit of life evolution. Under the command of the yet unexplained genetic program that natural selection put up in our brain, the spontaneous design of the neuronal software receives permanent input from the environment and uses it to make further rules out of every new relevant experience. That dynamic combination of instructions and memories becomes our self—the de-facto manager of everything we do.

Our symbolic identity connects so intimately with our physical individuality that *we* cannot tell them apart; they seem one single whole because they exchange messages incessantly. A super-simplified description of events would be as follows: The neuronal software gives instructions to our whole body and stores memories in the brain; the body interacts with the environment, executes instructions, and sends collected information back to the brain. When relevant, the neuronal program self-updates with the collected experience. Very dynamic during childhood and adolescence, the self-modification process slows down after maturity and moves backward as we approach death.

Unexpected actions—eating too much, drinking alcohol, changing fears into hatreds, frightening for no reason—confuse our neuronal software. Our software cannot tell right or natural from wrong or unnatural and, therefore, it adjusts its code to process the new events as if they were normal. Hence, harmful mental formations integrate into our neuronal program as redundant ego.

The essential self is what is left of our inflated self when we suppress the redundant portion. The essential self is also the *constant operating* self of those exceptional individuals with *inborn resistance* to harmful formations; such people never need to meditate and their self never inflates. Neither essential selves nor redundant egos are clear-cut entities. They are as abstract and diffuse as the *size of the self* discussed earlier, or as the *size of the wind,* with which it was compared.

The essential self, actual or potential, is a characteristic of every individual and there is no standard behavior in people acting out from their essential self. After somebody silences his or her harmful mental formations, his or her wholesome mental formations, which are different for each person, remain active.

An essential self is one with no harmful mental formations' influence either because the *owner* made them powerless, or they never tainted his/her brain in the first place. The self—be it the inflated self of most of us, the essential self after removing the stains of harmful formations, or the essential self of the few blessed whose self never contaminated—directs our actions no matter how much free will we claim to exercise.

In other words, we always act out from our *current* self, the inflated one, or the essential one (if our redundant self is null). The self of every moment is what rules our life. The self is always the chief in-charge and the way the self operates never changes. When we say *I, me or mine*, it is our symbolic identity talking, regardless the size of the self.[71] How is our behavior different in the two scenarios, the one driven by a contaminated self versus the one generated by the essential self? This will be discussed next.

Inflated Self versus Essential Self

Our inflated self does not know there is such a thing as an essential self. When our inflated self—essential self plus redundant ego—is in command, our cravings, aversions and biased views embed in the operating instructions of our sense of identity, and the inflated self plays the roles of both judge and jury. When we are greedy, rancorous or prejudiced, we see nothing abnormal in such behaviors because our inflated self, which determines what we do and think every minute, accepts and endorses them. "God made me so," we might say in order to imply the backing of some superior being.

When we operate from the inflated self, the things we crave, the objects for which we feel aversion or the biased views we are willing to fight for are all different manifestations of attachment. Such attachments, however, do not come from something within us deciding or marking them as ours; they are all artificial mental formations. Metaphorically speaking, on the contrary, our belongings own us; our hatreds slave our feelings; our opinions determine our thoughts.

Pertaining opinions, our inflated self is righteous and inflexible; our opinions—our political or religious views—do not admit challenges; they are unquestionable truths and everything else is wrong.

Though the essential self longs for freedom, it is weak, compared to the power of the inflated self, and it does not struggle much for its yearnings all the time. Occasionally the essential self catches a glimpse of our dependences and we may admit, "I should eat less, I should be more tolerant with that person, my opinions might be wrong." Soon, however, the inflated self hits our head and silently tells us who the boss is. This is why we fail to accomplish our year-end resolutions; there is no autonomous *I* to make a start. Because of its design, the inflated self never acts against its own rules.

Still it is through those glimpses that the essential self, through a sort of peaceful rebellion, may eventually take over. Unless this happens, our inflated self will rule our lives forever.

Mindfulness is permanent awareness and awareness is a quality of the essential self. The redundant ego is not— cannot be—aware of the damages it inflicts on us. Meditation and mindfulness are the habits we must implement to carry out this personal revolution; the decision to meditate and the actual practice of mindfulness are actions of our essential self. We—our essential self—must develop mindfulness to give a boost to the weaponry we are to use in our battle against mental formations.

Through observation of the harmful formations, mindfulness weakens them. When we are mindful, be it for minutes or hours, we operate from our essential self; this means we are able to see harmful formations as if they were outside; in fact, they are outside the essential self. Those are the moments when we—the word *we* means now our essential self—acknowledge the power of mindfulness, recognize the possibility to improve it through meditation, and undertake the path toward freedom. With patience and tenacity, we will succeed; this is a straightforward line of attack.

When we reach victory and start operating from our essential self, harmful mental formations lose their power over us— they become dormant neuronal code—because our strengthened inhibitory circuits maintain them inactive. From there on, our self is only essential self—the redundant ego is sleeping—and our attachments disappear.

INNER HARMONY

We already know that harmful formations, which sit in the code of our redundant ego, are the origin of anxiety-and-stress. When we silence cravings, aversions and biased views—when we deflate our inflated self—our essential self takes back the control that ideally should never have been lost; then suffering ends and we experience inner harmony. In other words, the redundant ego is the territory where the roots of suffering are seeded; the essential self is the land where inner harmony flourishes.

Chapter 13 – Toward Liberation

Transformation

Lifestyle changes, such as stopping an addiction, cultivating a new habit, initiating a new job or starting meditation, are transformational processes. During the initial steps, life changes demand certain adjustments in our knowledge, our skills and our attitudes; throughout the whole process, they require our permanent, strong determination. These four items—knowledge, skills, attitudes and determination—are the agents of personal change.

The materialization of new behaviors requires the learning or unlearning of pieces of knowledge, the adoption or stopping of certain skills or practices, and the development or abandonment of some attitudes. These three steps and the implementation of the desired change demand, from beginning to end, the decisive determination of the change pursuers, that is, their emotional obligation and drive to initiate, carry out and complete the required tasks.

An example should help to explain the workings of these agents. If we drink in excess and want to stop the habit, which is an unlearning process, we must do, undo or redo a few things, and act earnestly and zealously to leave the addiction behind. Things are not as simple as an emotional resolution today that, from tomorrow on, we will implement to drink never again. People who have faced drinking problems know well that this particular project calls for many laborious tasks and duties that go far beyond good intentions. The corrective actions, in any case, must happen fast.

The following list contains examples of actions and suppressions to control drinking; this list is not, in any way, a recipe or a procedure to deal with alcoholism. We must acknowledge our alcohol dependence and become aware of the harms of drinking (health issues, social problems, drunk driving, etc.); we should stop visiting bars or hanging out with drinkers—the socializing *skill*; and we should put behind the pseudo-gains of drinking, such as confidence, congeniality or extroversion.

The application of the change agents is rather stepwise. Knowledge comes first, that is, we learn that drinking affects all dimensions in our life—health, family, work, etc. Skills are next. We learn and practice what we should do: We must not buy liquor, go to bars, or interact with drinkers; we should learn to say, "No, thanks" whenever somebody offers us the first drink; we should openly acknowledge our problems with alcohol; we should give away the bottles we have at home; we may attend Alcoholics Anonymous meetings.

Attitudes come third. We should advertise to ourselves that we are stopping the habit and are welcoming the idea of being abstemious; we should remain attentive to the advantages of not drinking (save money, have more time for family and other activities, sleep longer hours, have no hangovers), and get used to the idea that drunken people are disgusting.

After we have reset knowledge, skills and attitudes, we are ready for the new or the modified behavior. The personal determination that we already exercised with the first three steps confronts now the toughest challenge: Stop drinking forever. This is the new behavior; when we adopt it, we will function, safely and successfully, in a new, different way.

How do books help in personal change implementation? Regardless the kind of change we may be considering, books' power of influence decreases as we go through the four change agents. Good writing may deliver the plain knowledge required by the change, the instructional portion of the skills, and hopefully the enthusiasm and motivation required by the undertaking. This is the farthest books can accompany the aspirants; beyond this point, change candidates depend exclusively on themselves.

13. Toward Liberation

The Agents and the Path

The path of mindfulness is a transformation toward a state of no suffering, which spontaneously evolves into a state of inner harmony. The elimination or reduction of suffering, as already written several times, requires the destruction of its roots, that is, the elimination of cravings, the termination of aversions and the ending of biased opinions.

Cravings, aversions and biased opinions are the harmful mental formations we are to stop—that we have to undo. In the process, however, we are not aiming at a new specific way of being or living that would meet certain predefined rules or circumstances. No, the change that comes from the exercise of mindfulness is the elimination of cravings, aversions and biased views; that is all. The behavior that so evolves, a life with no suffering, manifests within each person as his or her inner harmony that every individual will perceive and enjoy in his or her way.

As abstemious individuals behave and look as just those who do not drink, people without anxiety-and-stress behave and look as those who simply do not suffer. The abstemious-to-be person does not have to plan a different life; the *new life,* with better relationships, improved performance, enhanced finances and so on will happen automatically when his or her drinking stops.

Similarly, the traveler on the path of mindfulness does not need to set goals or create visions for a different existence; the new life of inner harmony, with no suffering, will just happen when cravings, aversions and biased views stop. What the traveler does need to do is to put in action the four change agents—knowledge, skills, attitudes and determination; the transformation comes spontaneously. We will describe how this goes for each agent in the following paragraphs.

Knowledge: Before we make the decision to eliminate our anxiety-and-stress, we have to acquaint ourselves with two

131

kinds of knowledge. One, which comes from outside, is the understanding of suffering, which we may get from a book like this one, a teacher, a seminar or another source. The other comes from within, we have to acknowledge such suffering by direct observation of our feelings and mental states.

Anxiety-and-stress has already been covered in sufficient detail. By now, we should well know about its reality, its origins, the real possibility of stopping or reducing it by cutting off its roots, and the application of mindfulness to eradicate such roots. The difficulty with anxiety-and-stress is that, though almost everybody undergoes it, most of us tend to deny it.

The acceptance of suffering is self-knowledge, something that nobody can teach us. The solution of any trouble begins with its acceptance; we cannot solve a problem that we deny exists. If we are going to fight a battle, we must first recognize that we have an enemy. If we do not accept the presence of suffering in our lives, the undertaking of a project to ameliorate the situation is a meaningless endeavor. Suffering is a background feeling and, as such, only each person experiences its effects. People go through anxiety-and-stress in their own way and every person has a different level of tolerance.

We never run out of excuses for uncomfortable circumstances—I work better under pressure, a certain level of stress is healthy, this headache is temporary, or that was just a moment of bad mood; knowledge, as an agent of change, invites us again to have a close look into the mirror of our feelings and our relationships.

Skills: Mindfulness is the skill—the ability—we should develop to control cravings, aversions and biased opinions. Meditation, in turn, is the tool we should use—the technique we should learn and apply—to improve such skill.

13. Toward Liberation

The instructions to use the tool are quite simple; this book contains the guidelines that the interested candidates may follow for their practice. This is particularly true for those people who already have experience with sitting meditation. However, as said earlier, the initial guidance of an honest teacher will always prove beneficial.

We tend to resist meditation with all kind of objections. The randomness, dispersion and involuntary nature of our thoughts are the most common excuses that we come up with to justify our resistance to undertaking meditation. Ironically, these are the best reasons why we should initiate the practice. In the *Determination* paragraph below there are other explanations that we fabricate for not meditating.

Mindfulness comes with meditation: The more we meditate, the more mindful we become, the less damage harmful formations do to us, the more we benefit from meditation... This becomes a virtuous circle after we meditate for some time with sufficient dedication and resolution (*sufficient* is also different for each person and may require lots of hours or days for most people).

At some point, mindfulness will become *meditation in action,* which means that, while we are being mindful, we are exercising the skill.

Attitudes: As the saying goes, we will carry out any task as long as we have enough reasons to perform it; we just need to find such reasons and act accordingly. Motives drive attitudes: the more crucial the motive, the more determined the attitude. The project to begin meditation and the process of making it a habit require an open, receptive attitude; we must find the appealing good reasons or incentives, and feel the intense needs or drivers that will definitely move us into action.

This book intends to provide some of the incentives that should pull us to mindfulness through meditation. The sources of the recommendations span over millennia. In the old times, the Buddha not only advocates meditation, but he also comes up with extensive details on how we should stay mindful. Twenty-five centuries later, cognitive sciences are confirming the soundness of the Buddha's recommendations and identifying the neurological workings that explain its benefits. These two heavyweight backings prove very convincing for the rational candidates who might be interested in meditation.

In addition to the old wisdom of the Sage and the modern research of the academics, the increasing media attention to all kinds of stress management techniques, with mindfulness meditation at the top of the rankings, is also a third encouraging element to start our meditation project. The media coverage is such that it may awaken our interest or, at least, our curiosity about mindfulness.

The incentives described above, which somehow attract us to meditation, come from knowledge, the first agent of change. Incentives emphasize what we will gain if we do something; they rest on something agreeable such as the inner harmony that we will experience through the practice of mindfulness, as has happened to other people.

Drivers, on the other hand, are those gun-type spurs that move us out from where we are now; their emphasis is not on some pleasure that we will enjoy later but some throbbing ache we want to evade now. The action drivers of mindfulness come from the anxiety-and-stress that is hurting us today.

The following story illustrates the differences between behavior drivers that demand action as opposed to incentives that encourage it.[72] A skeptic once asked a Buddhist teacher, "What have you gained through meditation?" The teacher replied, "Nothing at all." With that answer, the skeptic was even more doubtful: "Then what good is it?" "Let me tell you," the teacher explained, "what I lost through meditation: sickness, anger, depression, insecurity, the burden of old age, the fear of death. That is the good of meditation, which leads to the freedom from suffering."

Anxiety-and-stress is the kind of intensive need that should move us into meditating; we must acknowledge it, however. When we do so, we understand firsthand its reality and then that teacher's advice becomes our self-knowledge.

When we put together the incentives of the possibility to end suffering (knowledge received from outside) with the anxiety-and-stress as experienced directly by us (knowledge learned from within), we will have in our hands and brain the right attitude to start meditating, seriously, with the dedication and resolve that each person may require.

Determination: Once we know what to do, we master the skills to do it, and we have the proper attitude to do it, we are ready for the definitive action. The shift from mindlessness to mindfulness, though progressive and slow, is going to be much less difficult than what we originally thought; it may even be spontaneous in many cases. From start to finish— from the gaining of required knowledge, through the practice of the right skills and the development of the proper attitudes, to the adoption of both meditation and mindfulness— we need determination.

As said above, the dispersed mind is the first excuse we make up to evade meditation. The second most common pretext is the lack of time; such excuse is also the best test for our determination. The way we set priorities, deliberately or unconsciously, determines the sequence of most everything we do in our daily life. Somehow, we have to work around our priority rules to make room for meditation; three approaches may help us to accomplish this.

In the hierarchy of human needs,[73] the physiological ones are the most urgent, the safety needs come second, and the belongingness and love needs, the social needs, rank third. The physiological necessities include food, shelter and sleep; safety refers to qualities such as protection, health and employment; and the social needs involve relationships such as family, love and friends.

The first potential approach to open time for meditation resides in our social needs. While physiology and safety are mandatory—we are in trouble if we do not satisfy their associated requirements—some of the ingredients that lubricate our social relationships might be discretionary. Though the prioritization process is subjective, off-the-job items, such as sports, hobbies, memberships, parties and other leisure activities, are good candidates to match their priority against meditation.

The second approach is increasing the importance we assign to meditation versus other activities. Health, an element of the safety needs, is an area that does give weight to meditation; its benefits—the fact that it might help satisfy health as a safety need—are an important factor to take into account when prioritizing and planning our overall range of activities.

The third approach is to review our mental formations and the time load they are for us. In this respect, mental formations are a complex issue because they are part of the problem of not having time to meditate, yet their elimination is the solution we are looking for.

Mental formations, without *our explicit authorization*, manipulate our priorities and sneak in their preferences ahead of more rational choices. Unconsciously, the activities that fulfill our cravings, the actions we take to avoid the objects of our aversions, or the dedication to the likes and dislikes of our biased views, use a good deal of our already limited time.

To begin with, the satisfaction of cravings and addictions consumes long hours. Habits, such as drinking, smoking, overeating, watching television, gossiping and chitchatting, are examples of many compulsive behaviors that we could easily omit.

In less extent, the actions to evade the objects or circumstances of our aversions or phobias are also time consuming; such avoidances decrease our productivity and, therefore, they become wasters of time. If we fear flying, we may drive instead; if we hate highways, we take secondary roads; if that person is going to the meeting, we skip it though it was important to us.

Finally, because of our opinions, we spend hours attending meetings, watching sports matches, participating in ceremonies, supporting ideologies, arguing about our views, etc. Such activities tend to become addictive and therefore time and resource consuming.

If we apply mindfulness to our mental formations—if in the flashes of our essential self we become aware of mental formations, we might be able to deactivate them and free time for meditation. Being mindful permanently is difficult for the scattered mind but easy for the concentrated one. Scattering comes from mental formations and we can plan *mental stops* to review them. Strangely enough, these glimpses of mindfulness (the solution we are looking for) help in the solution of the problem (the lack of time to meditate) and improve our determination to undertake meditation and mindfulness.

The third pretext to evade meditation is the intrinsic difficulty of its practice, difficulty that results from the second excuse—our distracted, elusive mind. Though the subject was already covered, we want to emphasize that determination is equally required to prevail over this barrier. When we acknowledge the dispersion of our mind, and we somehow spare time for the practice, then we must commit ourselves to stay on, regardless how boring, frustrating or tough we find the exercise at the beginning.

Determination is the most critical agent of any transformation. When we are committed, we will do whatever it takes to materialize the other three key ingredients—knowledge, skills and attitudes.

The Paradoxes

There are a couple of paradoxes associated with mindfulness. The first one comes from the perceived difficulty of mindfulness when compared with the easy-to-follow instructions of the nonjudgmental observation of something—the observation of our body, our sensations and our mental states. The second paradox is the contrast between the same high degree of difficulty perceived by most people and the ease of the practice for a minority.

Let us start with the first paradox. The path of mindfulness consists of two components—periodic meditation and permanent awareness—intimately connected, still independent. This independence is what makes walking the path a quite manageable endeavor.

Meditation supports mindfulness. As we increase the frequency and duration of our meditation sessions (the first component), mindfulness (the second component) becomes more and more natural. While we do need to allocate specific time to meditate—time we often claim we cannot spare, we put mindfulness into effect in real time, concurrently with all our daily activities. If anything, mindfulness *gains* time for us, because our awareness makes us more effective in our daily activities.

The bulk of our determination, therefore, must go to meditation both for starting the habit—acquiring the knowledge, developing the skills, working on the attitudes—and for holding on to its continuous practice afterward. Our acknowledgement of our anxiety-and-stress, our intimate understanding of its roots, our recognition of the possibility of destroying such roots and our acceptance of the feasibility to end suffering are the ingredients that lead the required determination. By making mindfulness easy, our successful determination to meditate resolves our first paradox.

The fact that many people consider mindfulness difficult and some find it very easy and natural is the second paradox. A well-known sixth century text, *The Verses on the Faith Mind*,[74] one of the most profound and shortest writings of Eastern thought, explains both paradoxes. The opening lines of the text, a wonderful summary of what this author calls Pragmatic Buddhism, state:

> The Path[75] is not difficult
> for those who have no preferences.
> When cravings and aversions are both absent
> everything becomes perfectly clear.
> Make the smallest distinction, however,
> and heaven and earth are set infinitely apart.
> If we wish to see the truth,
> we hold no opinions for or against anything.
> The struggle between what we like against what we
> dislike is the disease of the mind.
> When we do not understand the deep meaning of things,
> our inner harmony is disturbed to no avail.

The first sentence—the Path is not difficult—seems to contradict the high level of determination that meditation demands; we would expect that easy endeavors should not demand much dedication. The second line, however, establishes the requisite for the path to be easy, which is having no preferences. Having no preferences is the result of the stopping—the letting go—of cravings, aversions and biased views. This is what meditation does; it helps us to let go. Once we appease harmful mental formations, the Path becomes easy. The disease of mind that comes from the struggle of likes and dislikes is suffering. As long as we do not understand anxiety-and-stress, its roots, its removal, and the way to remove it, we will not experience inner harmony.

These few lines are a fine compendium of what this book has covered at length.

As Saint Theresa says referring to mental prayer, with repeated practice the exercise will become progressively easier. We should listen to the Catholic nun's advice (the process is similar though her purposes are different) and keep meditating methodically. Our determination will pay out and, as we start reaping the benefits, meditating will become an effortless routine. Then, when we stop having preferences, the path of mindfulness—and the path of *The Verses on the Faith Mind* quoted above—will be easy. This explains our second paradox.

Chapter 14 – Undertaking Meditation

Things to Do and Things to Avoid

People who have reached this far in their reading, meditators and non-meditators alike, are almost certainly giving serious consideration to start up mindfulness meditation as the next, natural move toward mindfulness. What should they do? Where should they begin?

This section goes over again the recommendations that beginners should follow in the meditation practice itself as well as discusses the considerations they should take into account regarding the selection of teachers and schools.

The techniques: The practice of meditation has already been explained in much detail; in spite of this coverage, it is fitting to emphasize again the importance of the use of appropriate anchors. Out of the four basic guidelines, mindfulness meditation shares the first three requirements with many other approaches to meditation: a quiet environment, a passive attitude and a comfortable sitting posture. The kind of items on which meditators should focus their attention (the fourth guideline) is what sets mindfulness meditation substantially apart.

The application of the proper anchors is instrumental for the development of our mindfulness skill. During our practice, we should maintain the focus of attention on anchors around our breath or our sensations. While the attention to our breath is straightforward—we all breathe in the same way, the observation of sensations does offer a number of alternatives, which are acceptable for the practice. Three common approaches are:

1. We may observe sensations as they come and go throughout our body.

2. We may focus attention on a specific spot on our body.

3. Or we may rotate our attention around the whole body, noticing either the type of sensations we are feeling at each part (pleasant, unpleasant or neutral; gross or subtle), or the absence of sensations (when this happens).

The anchors and techniques described above are everything we need to start meditating; they perfectly do the required work. Though beginners might feel tempted to use other body and sensations' anchors,[76] their list must be as short as possible so that meditation instructions remain simple.

The emphasis on the short-list recommendation increases sharply with respect to other kinds of anchors. We should avoid the application of any meditational devices or tricks that are unrelated to our body or our sensations; more specifically, meditators are strongly discouraged from using mantras, chants, background music, fragrances, prayers, rosaries, figures, images or any other element of religious, paranormal, mythological, magical or power-inducing content.

Schools and teachers: The contents of the previous heading on the techniques around meditation had already been covered in previous chapters. The reason to revisit the subject is that the four guidelines of mindfulness meditation provide the best criteria for new students to look for and select both schools and teachers. If new students want to learn mindfulness meditation, the technique being taught at a school or by some teacher must match those four basic guidelines on environment, attitude, posture and anchors.

The elaboration on this recommendation opens room for some further advice. To begin with, students should work their initial sessions with the assistance of teachers who are experienced meditators. Meditation is not a fixed-length program as the courses we take in college; instead, it is a continuous activity for the rest of our lives. The way we initiate the practice will influence our future persistence, therefore we should start with the right foot.

The key factors in the selection of both meditation schools and teachers should be the transmission of the wisdom, virtue and discipline of the path of mindfulness (and, by extension, of mindfulness meditation). Eventually mindfulness will become a daily habit in our lives. Though most schools and teachers must take into consideration their financial conditions, which force them in most cases to charge for their lessons, monetary gain should not be the reason of existence of the school or the compelling purpose of the teacher's work.[77]

"Service comes first" is a common motto of many trades. Though such a business rule is ideally applicable to any product or service that we want to obtain, meditation training is a very special kind of *service* whose suppliers must provide beyond any profit consideration.

New meditators must keep in mind the vulnerability and risks that come from the altered mental states associated with meditation; accordingly, they must do their homework to identify good and honest prospective teachers. The guides to accomplish the task are the common sense directions we use when we are looking for any service; they include finding out what is available, interviewing the potential suppliers, and meeting people who are using the service.

How do we examine the staff of a school or the teacher under consideration? There is a simple rule: Both should aim at making their students independent, that is, making them self-reliant meditators as soon as possible; in other words, the recurring payments of trained students should not become a permanent source of income for the school. The independence from teachers must accompany the liberation from suffering. We should choose schools and teachers whose mission aims at students *flying solo*—the sooner, the better—so they are able to meditate daily on their own, wherever they are.

The main responsibility of their independence sits, however, on the students' shoulders. New students must aim at working by themselves as soon as feasible; the length of this period depends a lot on his or her perseverance. The high frequency demanded by the practice of meditation (as discussed next) makes extremely impractical and uneconomical the option of paid meditation lessons on a permanent basis.

Frequency and length: Two of the most common questions new students ask relate to the frequency of the practice and the duration of each session: For how long and how often should we meditate? We have two answers that both look evasive. The first one is, as long and as often as possible—the longer the better. This sounds not only too vague but also too challenging: Shall I meditate four hours a day? Obviously, the meaning of *possible* depends a lot on each person's priorities and denotes something different for everyone. The point to make is that for each person meditating should be a top priority activity; in fact, a life project.

The second answer returns the ball back to each potential meditator: The more cravings, aversions and biased opinions we have, and the more dispersed our mind, the more and longer we should meditate. We, and only we, can assess the magnitude of our anxiety-and-stress: The more *infecting* the harmful mental formations, the larger the dose of *antibiotics* required.

Beyond the above answers, this author refrains from recommending the duration of each meditation session. Every meditation school, mindfulness meditation or otherwise, usually offers some guideline, which ranges from some 20-30 minutes every session up to one hour. On the other hand, there is a general agreement on the frequency of the practice: Ideally, we should meditate twice a day, every day.

Is this level of dedication difficult? Yes. Does it demand a lot of determination? Yes. (By the way, beware of schools or teachers that offer dramatic results or miracles within a few weeks and with minimum dedication.) Determination is the cornerstone of the meditation project (and of any project).

Retreats and groups: We should do whatever possible to reinforce our determination. Two strategies, the attendance to meditation retreats and the association with regular meditators,[78] prove helpful in this direction. Both are lines of attack commonly used to dive deep into mindfulness and to stimulate exchange of information on the subject; it is good to learn that our struggles with the practice are not exclusively ours.

Attending training retreats as the first step to learn meditation is an approach that beginners should always consider; after participating in a several-day intensive program, students should perceive the benefits of mindfulness almost immediately.

The importance assigned to practicing by ourselves does not conflict with the recommendation of being part of groups that get together to meditate. There is no need to elaborate more on these recommendations; they are self-explanatory and self-justifiable.

These two approaches do need, however, a word of caution: We must not search for retreats or friendships with other meditators through affiliation to any cult or sectarian group; we must indeed run away from any membership that seeds in our mind dependencies or biased views. Instead of freedom from suffering, they will bring us further slavery.

The Alternatives

The habit of mindfulness meditation favors the habit of mindfulness; meditation does train our brain to focus attention and to remain mindful of what happens within and around us for longer and longer periods. One-step further, the habit of mindfulness reduces our suffering and eventually liberates us from it. Linking the two premises, the continued practice of meditation should lead to the end of anxiety-and-stress—the most significant goal of meditation.

Two obvious questions arise: Is mindfulness meditation the only technique that sharpens awareness? Is mindfulness the only path toward the freedom from suffering? With some clarifications, the answer to both questions is negative, which, consequently, leads to the next inquiry: What are the options?

Alternatives to meditation: Let us begin with the alternatives to mindfulness meditation. In the broadest sense, as lifting weights with different routines prepares people for all kinds of muscle-demanding tasks, a broad set of mental concentration techniques should help us to become more attentive to the wide variety of events and thoughts that flood our daily living.

This author may say, from direct experience, that mindfulness meditation does the work—it does lead to the *advertised* results of improving mindfulness. Nevertheless, anyone who has successfully applied other techniques, whatever they are, may also express the same claim. Since, from a pragmatic point of view, truth is what produces results, the value of mindfulness meditation for anybody will only become their truth when they realize and experience by themselves the effectiveness of this very technique to improve mindfulness and enjoy its benefits.

Though this book puts forward some excluding guidelines—the do not's of the previous section, no *concentration enhancing* technique should be disqualified. If someone is gaining tangible benefits from certain practices, he or she should keep taking advantage of them.

Many people, using a variety of mental and physical exercises, often have immediate, short-range objectives; they want to gain something and they want it soon. Examples of these techniques are yoga, tai chi, biofeedback and many other versions of meditation (such as transcendental meditation). The most commonly expected outcomes are stress reduction, health improvement and performance enhancement. While the ultimate goal of mindfulness meditation is freedom from suffering, many people do undertake mindfulness meditation with short-term expectancies.

Whatever we do to improve our awareness—and thus mindfulness—is a step in the right direction to reduce anxiety-and-stress; there is some common ground between mindfulness meditation and those other practices. In fact, many new meditators with experience in other concentration techniques generally adjust easier to the initial demands of mindfulness meditation.

In summary, there are alternative approaches, other than mindfulness meditation, to improve our concentration skills and produce some near-term gains. Nevertheless, this book neither endorses nor bans any of such methods for mindfulness enhancement; however, it does categorically recommend mindfulness meditation as an effective technique for such purpose. Once more, the reasons behind such emphasis are (1) the simplicity and straightforwardness of the focusing anchors, and (2) the absolute independence from any doctrine or sect.

If something else works for some people, however, they should keep doing it. Any practice—any system or therapy—that leads to the desired results without chaining the practitioner to any sect, cult, master or financial obligation is good.

Alternatives to mindfulness: While meditation is an exercise that we should practice as often and long as possible, mindfulness is a permanent habit; ideally, we should remain mindful every second we are awake. The habit of meditation is a habit similar to playing a sport or going to concerts, which we do not do all the time. We have to interrupt everything else when we meditate, play baseball or go to the concert hall.

There might be alternatives to the techniques that we use to improve our faculty of awareness but there is no equivalent state to being mindful—we are mindful (sharply attentive, conscious, aware…) or our mind is dispersed (scattered, distracted, sidetracked…).

Ineffectual Recommendations

The benefits of meditation and mindfulness have been discussed extensively; whatever the actual gains are, it is not possible to pinpoint whether one habit, the other, or both, are the actual source of the materialized progress. Some positive mental states and behaviors, however, are apparent to us and even to others. When this happens, we are fully aware of our life, just as it is unfolding. Is the beauty of these instants the result of mindfulness? We do not think so; this beauty is mindfulness itself, as it was first defined.

Following are some examples of what happens when we are mindful: We do not feel resentment or hatred toward anybody; we forgive and forget offenses and insults; we experience calm and relaxation; we maintain balance; we may serenely tolerate long waits and lose track of time; we seem to carry our duties with minimum effort; and most everything seems to be working fine. Second arrows do not hit us when we are mindful.

These behaviors are noticeable and we tend to assign positive adjectives to the individuals who display such qualities: loving, forgiving, calm, poised, tolerant, genuine, agreeable… Obviously, if we would like to become loving, forgiving, poised, tolerant, genuine or agreeable, what do we need to do? The TV, radio, magazine and church counselors have the answer: Do everything exactly as those (loving, forgiving, calm, etc.) people do; follow their tracks. Is that right? Wrong!

Friends and family who watch TV, listen to radio, read magazines and go to church, love to provide similar advice. Should we mention to them any emotional trouble we might be going through (sadness, anger, jealousy, hatred, partiality...), or display bad character for a moment, they become expert therapists. They soon come with the best-intentioned advice that they read about or heard recently; it is also the most ineffectual, useless guidance. In the following lines, there are a few comments on some of these frequent recommendations that we might have heard recently.

Forgive! Forget! The offenses we are to forgive and the events we are to forget are bad memories that trigger aversions to real or imaginary things or events. Mindfulness will facilitate the stopping of the automatic negative reactions whenever the bad memories arise. Forgiving and forgetting do not come from neuronal excitatory circuits that turn off but from inhibitory circuits that turn on. We cannot make the decision and take the action to forgive or forget in the same way we choose a restaurant and go there for lunch.

Calm down! Maintain balance! Calmness and poise come from mental quietness. We do not command our brain to be silent. To calm down and maintain balance, we should stop the noisy mental formations that are disturbing us.

Live in the present! Our brain does not perceive time; our brain constructs time—past, present and future—as it creates our sense of identity. As mindfulness sizes down the redundant ego, our dependency of time loses strength. Our present is the motions and postures of our body, the sensations we perceive in it, and the mental states we experience. When we are mindful, our essential self is in command; living in present time is an outcome, not an intention.

Be spontaneous! Flow with life! We cannot be spontaneous when we act out from our redundant ego. When the redundant ego is in control, cravings, aversions and biased opinions make all decisions for us; we do not even notice. Our redundant ego distorts what would otherwise be our natural, spontaneous behavior; we can only be spontaneous when our actions come from a harmful-mental-formations-free, essential self; at that stage, life actually flows. We cannot be spontaneous on purpose.

Accept things as they are! What move us out from acceptance are both the cravings for what we lack, or those things we do have but want more of, and the aversions to what actually or imaginarily surround us. Acceptance is the absence of cravings and aversions. As mindfulness places mental formations at bay, we take things as they are. Again, we cannot decide to accept something that our harmful mental formations are rejecting.

The previous criticism does not mean that we should always scorn the above well-intended pieces of advice; they might have some cheering content and open up channels for inter-communication and self-observation, which is good. When we put a smile on our face, we will feel better than with the frown we had a few seconds before. However, motivational speeches are not—cannot be—alternatives to meditation or mindfulness; they have different purposes.

Chapter 15 – Pure Awareness

Surrendering to the Experience

As already said, students must approach meditation with no expectation of any kind. This section and the next one might possibly create some unsettling aspirations that could lead to frustration or confusion. This is why this chapter has been placed toward the end of the book. Readers must put aside any personal desire or goal they develop about their meditation practice as they go through this material.

When somebody begins a meditation session, he or she often starts with an agitated mind, showered by a variety of external and internal stimuli, many of them unwanted or unnoticed. With different degrees of intensity, the five hindrances to mindfulness (greed, hostility, sloth, restlessness and doubt) are often present, weakening when not deterring the intention to meditate.

By the very act of scheduling the session and sitting, meditators leave sloth and doubt behind, at least for the moment. By choosing and favoring physical isolation—quiet place, eyes closed, passive attitude, comfortable posture— meditators diminish external stimuli. Through mental isolation—they direct attention to their breath or their sensations—meditators put greed, hostility and restlessness under control.

This is everything meditators need to do. During their practices for the rest of their lives, meditators can stay in level zero, the mental state any student with some perseverance will reach; this level zero is actual, effective, functional mindfulness meditation. Such actions—sitting, isolating, directing thought—take only minutes, if not seconds. From here on, meditators should also maintain their attention on the anchor of their choice, to which they recurrently return every time their mind goes somewhere else. However minuscule all these actions, meditators do things; they are *active* subjects.

Does anything else come next? The answer is no and yes. It is negative because focusing attention on their anchors, holding it there, and pulling attention back when distracted is the whole story. The answer, however, is also positive because of the things that, with perseverance, meditators might experience after some time (here *after some time* means both some minutes after beginning a session and a few days, weeks or even months after starting meditation on a regular basis). These things—these new events—switch to *passive* the *active* role that meditators have exercised so far; now they become submissive observers that surrender to the experience.

Flow of Sensations

When students are constant and persistent enough with their meditation, and are able to stay in level zero in every session (that is, they have maintained focus on their anchors repeatedly and consistently), their practice evolves into more insightful experiences. What are these new experiences?

Without following any specific technique, practitioners enter deeper meditative levels, that is, more inner-focused states. During those states, meditators increasingly perceive subtle, generally pleasant sensations either in isolated parts of the body or as a flow that runs throughout it, and then they enter some very special mental states. The isolated pleasant sensations and their flow come spontaneously; there are no instructions to prompt them. The Buddha speaks about four absorptions—four levels of meditative states.

Meditators must not go after these absorptions, and must not be concerned about which level they are entering, or whether they do or do not enter any of these states. To avoid the possible frustration or confusion mentioned in the opening paragraph of this chapter, it is opportune to review the definition given earlier. Mindfulness meditation is a mental exercise during which practitioners with their eyes gently closed, sit in a comfortable position in a quiet environment, adopt a passive attitude and focus attention on certain anchors in order to enhance their daily awareness. Level zero is mindfulness meditation; it is good enough for anybody to stay at that level.

Given the uniqueness—the very personal nature—of these absorptions, each meditator will probably describe his or her experience in a different manner. The Buddha explains the four absorptions as follows[79] (see also "Meditation beyond Anchors" in Appendix 2):

Joy: When meditators let greed, hostility, restlessness, sloth and doubt—the hindrances to meditation and mindfulness—go, they start perceiving pleasant sensations and, as they may move their attention throughout their body, the pleasant sensations follow. When this happens, they enter the first meditative state, a state of subtle but real joy.

Physical and mental calm: When meditators center awareness on this new sensory experience, there comes to be an undirected, spontaneous flow of pleasant sensations. Meditators experience joy, free from directed thought (free from anchors), and enter a second meditative state, a state of physical and mental calm. Conscious of this state, meditators are just attentive to the flow of sensations, wherever in the body they are present, with no intent to qualify them.

Equanimity: When meditators, remaining attentive and open to their whole experience, maintain awareness on the broad array of sensations they are feeling, and become indifferent to the joy they are experiencing, they enter a third state, a state of equanimity and impartial calm, and stay fully conscious and lucid of this equanimity.

Pure awareness: When meditators, sharply attentive and neutral to any sensation or feeling they may perceive, are aware of the full span of their attention with no judgment

153

over pleasure or pain, meditators enter a fourth state, an even deeper state of pure awareness. They become aware of the silence in their mind and their consciousness is open to the experience. All feelings and perceptions are fresh and new, and they are not compared with any knowledge or previous event.

The previous paragraphs deserve some comments. First, we should not interpret the above narrative to the letter.[80] The descriptions of the absorptions are signs of direction, not yardsticks; definitions of mental states are elusive and vague if not inaccurate.

Second, a consequence of the first point, we should not pursue or try to imitate something that is not straightforward; however appealing joy, physical and mental calm, equanimity or pure awareness are, we should not sit in meditation expecting to reach them. While we should not strive for the absorptions as described, we may welcome them as they *show up* and detachedly observe and enjoy the experience. There are no well-defined boundaries between one state and the next, and each meditator may sort them out differently. We should think of pure awareness, the deepest of the four levels, as an ideal state, which will eventually manifest without us pursuing it.

Third, meditators will learn that, with dedication and time, their mind will become progressively more calm and their awareness increasingly sharper. Again, the experience of mindfulness meditation is very personal. Whatever meditative states a meditator enters and however he or she chooses to name them, when distractions come (and they will, though less and less frequently), practitioners go back to level zero and start working again with their anchors.

Fourth, in the level of joy (the first one), as the meditator uses the body's parts as rotating anchors, the pleasant sensations follow attention. In the level of physical and mental calm (the second one), the meditator, free from directed thought, stops the use of anchors and their attention moves, with no particular intention or plan, toward the parts of the body where he or she is experiencing pleasant sensations; that is, attention spontaneously follows sensations.

Fifth, a repetition for the purpose of emphasis, meditators must not try to repeat this narrative or a similar one; such intention will only lead to confusion, frustration and, in the worst case, to giving up meditation. Simply staying in level zero will improve by itself the faculty of awareness.

Are There Different Types of Mindfulness Meditation?

There are several techniques to focus awareness on fixed anchors (the breath, one point in the body or one specific sensation), or rotate attention on *moving* anchors (on different parts of the body, or on different sensations) but there is only one practice with no standard set of instructions. In our early practice of meditation, some directions, recorded or live, will always prove useful. As we gain experience, however, we simply sit to meditate with no particular plan or expectation in mind. Every session is the same recurring journey but we can walk a different trail every time.

Furthermore, from a different perspective, the focusing of attention on anchors (level zero) and the surrendering to the flow that follows (absorptions one to four) are not two different forms of meditation; instead, they are two stages of one single whole.[81]

In level zero, students mostly exercise awareness by using anchors to exclude distractions and unnecessary thoughts. In levels one to four, they forget about anchors and become attentive to everything that is going on in their body and their mind. As we move on in these levels, our awareness is more and more passive.

The frequency of students' brain activity during meditation's level zero is between eight to twelve cycles per second; the medical term for this frequency is *alpha rhythm*. As meditators enter the deeper levels of the practice (levels 1 to 4), the brain activity goes down to the so called *theta rhythm*, during which the frequency is between four to seven cycles per second (see endnote 64.)

Most meditators iterate back and forth between the two stages. They purposely go to stage one when they realize they are unfocused; they move to stage two spontaneously. Only extremely experienced meditators—the author's guess—stay in the upper levels for long uninterrupted periods.

Mindfulness meditation is a single, multifaceted exercise that develops and favors mindfulness; mindfulness meditation is a road with many lanes, mindfulness is a unique destination.

Still Body and Quiet Mind

Mindfulness meditation is not about controlling either the body or the mind; instead, mindfulness meditation is about stilling the body and quieting the mind. At pure awareness, the peak state of meditation, with the body as still as feasible, mindfulness meditation is a complete emptying of the mind. At that moment, when awareness is least contaminated and attention is sharpest, the mind releases anything that runs through it.

To get there we have to open both mind and body to the meditative experience. As we enter the flow, we stop working with anchors; we just use them to expel out whatever thoughts or distractions sporadically pop up.

We cannot promote or go after pure awareness; we are not to follow any instruction at all to arrive there. We just observe sensations when they are present and are aware of their absence when they are not. When our mind is silent, we know *our mind is silent* but we do not attach to the silence or command our mind to stay silent. Even the word *silence* makes noise.

There is no possible description for the experience of pure awareness. When we try to take a *verbal photograph* of those moments, with the intention to describe them in words later on, we are not there anymore. If we fall into this temptation to verbalize the experience, well... we focus attention on our breath. If we come to judge what is going on, or wonder what is next, or think we are spiritually done, or this is what the teacher said, or... then, what does the reader think we should do? As many times as necessary, we return our attention to our breath. The flow will then come back spontaneously.

It is inaccurate to say that meditators reach pure awareness; instead, pure awareness reaches meditators when they unlock hindrances and open wide the door to the experience. At that point, there is mental silence and the meditators' perception of time changes. This explains why some advanced practitioners can effortlessly meditate for many hours and stay in weeks-long retreats.

This is all this book dares to say about pure awareness. For an indescribable state, probably too much was said already.

The Merging of Meditation and Mindfulness

With our continuous and persistent practice of meditation, three things happen: (1) meditating becomes an easy, pleasant task and a habit—an instinct—that we do not have to force ourselves to find time for; (2) we enter the deeper mental levels of meditation described earlier and (3) our faculty of awareness expands. These improvements simply happen. While we should not feel jubilant about such progresses, we do notice them. On the other hand, we must not feel frustrated if they come slowly or do not seem to be coming at all; we simply keep practicing.

The development of our faculty of awareness opens up further options that snowball our mindfulness skills. The application of these options reinforce (they do *not* replace) our daily meditation sessions. We insist: We must meditate twice daily for as long as we are able to make time available.

Two common circumstances present wonderful opportunities for exercising our mindfulness skills. The first one occurs during our *passive* experiences; the second one takes place when we are performing *active* tasks, which we may be carrying out for personal reasons or in response to an external demand.

Passive experiences are those do-nothing or do-little periods during which our role is being spectators (as opposed to actors), and we do not need to apply much knowledge, skill or concentration; we are just there because it is part of something else. Listening to music, strolling, showering, waiting for something and travelling as passengers (not as drivers) are examples of this passivity.

Mindfulness is (and should be) a spontaneous habit. However, if we purposefully sharpen our attention on our body, sensations and mental states during passive events, while maintaining awareness of what is going on in the environment, we are up to a certain extent practicing both meditation and mindfulness. We can say that, at those moments, meditation and mindfulness fuse—they become one single act.

Things are different when we are carrying out some duty that requires knowledge, skills, tools and alertness. This time we are active subjects and our attention is (and must be) focused on what we are consciously doing while, simultaneously, we are aware of how our body and brain are doing the job, and what sensations and mental states are associated with it.

In this second case, we could extrapolate our meditation guidelines and *use* the activity being performed as a kind of *anchor* of the practice: Every time our mind goes somewhere else, we simply return attention to the task of the moment. In spite of the physical or mental motions involved in this active awareness, we could also think that, when we focus attention on the task and how our body and brain are performing it, a fusion also occurs between mindfulness and this kind of *dynamic* meditation.

The above two situations (which cover a good fraction of what we do during our waking hours) illustrate *the meditative nature of mindfulness* and *the mindful nature of meditation*. Meditation and mindfulness are intimately connected. This connection explains the apparent divergence on the views of two well-known Eastern sages, Japanese thirteenth-century Zen Buddhist sage Eihei Dōgen, the founder of the Sōtō school of Zen, and Indian philosopher J. Krishnamurti, the modern spiritual teacher quoted several times throughout this book.

Zazen, the sitting practice of Zen Buddhism that aims at calming body and mind, and at understanding the nature of existence, is a meditation approach similar in many aspects to mindfulness meditation. Dōgen says that zazen (meditation) is the ultimate practice, and students do not need to do anything other than sit to meditate. He adds that[82] "this is indeed the essential self; the nature of existence is not to be sought outside of this practice," a statement that clearly excludes any other mental developmental habit. For Dōgen, meditation is everything.

Krishnamurti is the other side of the coin. The Indian philosopher criticizes the use of meditation techniques, in general, and the exercises that focus attention on mental devices such as mantras, prayers, figures or saints, in particular. He says that when students learn a mind quieting technique, the mental trick (the mantra, the prayer, etc.) substitutes the real goal of the student's search (truth, peace, existential meaning...) and he or she end up affiliated to the teaching school or system that sponsors it.

Krishnamurti says,[83] "The beginning of mindfulness[84] is being aware of every movement of thought and feeling, knowing all the layers of consciousness." For him mindfulness is everything:[85] "Mindfulness is a state of mind, which looks at everything with complete attention, totally, not just parts of it. When you learn about yourself, watch yourself, watch the way you walk, how you eat, what you say, the gossip, the hate, the jealousy—if you are aware of all that in yourself, that is part of mindfulness."

Stressing determination, Dōgen seems to be saying, "meditate persistently, and you will stay mindful effortlessly"; emphasizing awareness, Krishnamurti is implying "be permanently mindful—attentive of your body, your sensations and your mental states; meditation techniques are useless when not damaging."

At this point, this author cannot resist the temptation to play with and reword a beautiful quote about those special individuals who make no distinction between work and play.[86] The paraphrase of the original line follows: "The masters in the art of living draw no sharp distinction between their mindfulness and their meditation. They hardly know which is which. They simply pursue the path toward the end of suffering through whatever they are doing and leave others to determine whether they are exercising mindfulness or practicing meditation. To themselves they always seem to be doing both."

Two things may be said about these wonderful people: On one hand, they are an extremely small minority. We, the rest of humanity, consider meditation and mindfulness as two different, complementary habits; while meditation strengthens our awareness skills, mindfulness facilitates meditation. We, the very large majority, need the exercise of mindfulness as well as the practice of meditation. On the other hand, privileged sages may not need the two practices; they are born either mindful, determined or both.

Chapter 16 – The Outcome

The Hidden Goal

As we cannot produce silence, so we cannot fabricate inner harmony. If we shut down the sources of the disrupting noises, however, we can facilitate the occurrence of silence and, entering through the back door, we are making it happen. Similarly, we can favor the emergence of inner harmony by turning off the origins of the mental noises—cravings, aversions and biased views—that lead to the dissonance of suffering.

Inner harmony is like a hidden destination toward which we cannot draw a route on a map. Instead, inner harmony is a kind of hidden place that we will certainly find on our path of mindfulness: the more we walk, the sooner inner harmony will show up.

How will we know if we find inner harmony? Mental states are difficult, sometimes impossible, to describe; everybody has trouble communicating their experience of feelings and moods. The same happens with inner harmony; its definition as an inner state that permits us to be at peace and act confidently, even in the face of difficulties, does provide a good idea of what it means but does not explain the actual experience.

The destination, in spite of being out of sight, is recognizable; when someone experiences inner harmony, he or she knows it. Since most everyone has gone through such wonderful moments—that season when everything within us seemed to be working smoothly, the occasion when we remained indifferent to someone's unfair verbal attacks, the time when we performed outstandingly in a task, the weeks during which we had that obsessive behavior under control—people have a good picture of what inner harmony is. Unfortunately, due to the recurrent attacks of cravings, aversions and biased views, those periods are shorter than we would like them to be—unless we become mindful.

Inner harmony does not have anything to do with success or accomplishments, neither does it depend on outside events. While inner harmony is not the possession or the presence of anything, good living or pleasant circumstances are not at odds with inner harmony. We do not need to renounce anything or run away from any situation to enjoy inner harmony. Since they are external, inner harmony has no conflict with assets or places; inner harmony's true conflict is with attachment. Attachment, inner harmony and suffering all happen within us. Inner harmony is not the presence of anything; inner harmony is the absence of anxiety-and-stress. Yes, we live better and perform more effectively when we are in inner harmony.

Equanimity, serenity and contentment are words that come close to inner harmony and help us to understand it. Leaving expressions aside, when we experience inner harmony, we know we are there and we are mindful of such mental state—of our indifference to cravings or aversions, our impartiality of views, our detachment from time or labels, our acceptance of everything... The very moment we become proud of any manifestation of inner harmony, we are again away from it.

Inner Harmony and Happiness

People often mistake happiness for inner harmony; the terms indeed have things in common but they are not synonyms. Everybody enjoying inner harmony is happy in his or her way, but happiness does not always imply inner harmony. On purpose, this book has avoided the subject of happiness up to now; still we want to cover it so that we do not leave readers with unanswered questions they surely would like to ask.

16. The Outcome

Happiness is a positive feeling; we all know that. But there are several problems with the denomination, not with the wonderful feeling. To begin with, it refers to too many inter-actions (relationships, jobs, possessions, etc.) and does not have the same meaning for everybody. Happiness may come from getting or accomplishing a variety of transactions (a love partner, a promotion, a new house, etc.) that come from outside and we consider positive. However great these events are, they do not translate into inner harmony.

Secondly, some events that make us temporarily happy orig-inate in the disturbers of inner harmony. For example, some may come from the satisfaction of cravings (e.g. an excellent meal) or the success of our biased views (e.g. the victory of our political party). In the worst cases, a *shameful* happiness may stem from the disgrace of someone for whom we feel aversion.

Furthermore, while we can look for happiness—most every-body does—we cannot and should not pursue inner harmony. We may obtain happiness, however fragile or momentary, by getting or achieving the gratifications that we are after; we reach inner harmony by removing the barriers that block its development. We must add things to get happiness; we have to subtract stuff to let inner harmony blossom.

Some spiritual teachers have opted for redefining happiness; since they consider it something well above ordinary gratifi-cations, they remove from its popular definition the mundane links commonly associated with material goods, and place the adjective *true* in front of *happiness*. Though they do not express it, this reduced version of happiness implies that whatever results from material satisfactions is not happiness. According to these thinkers, true happiness is within us and we will never find it out there, because *true happiness* does not and cannot depend upon external gratifications or condi-tions.

This author dislikes the expression *true happiness*; it opens room not only for confusion but also to the awkward contradiction of *false* or *fictitious* happiness. In spite of the reluctance to use the word, this true happiness resembles inner harmony. In the same order of ideas, unhappiness—sorrow, sadness, discontent, depression and so on—is also close to suffering.

Russian novelist Fyodor Dostoevsky[87] does not speak about inner harmony or anxiety-and-stress but he writes a lot about happiness and suffering. He thoughtfully says, "Man is unhappy because he does not know he is happy; only because of that. It is everything, everything! Whoever learns this will immediately become happy, that same moment."

This author dares to suggest a twist to this wonderful quote which the Russian genius might like. The adjusted interpretation explains a lot of what has been written so far. With the acquiescence of Master Dostoevsky, we do not—we cannot—learn that we are happy; still we can do something equivalent in two steps.

First, we must learn and understand the reality of suffering (and our predisposition to it); then, we must unlearn and forget that we are unhappy. How do we do this? By eliminating the cravings, aversions and biased opinions where all unhappiness and suffering originate.

The following metaphor, to close this section, provides a good picture of the difference between happiness and inner harmony. Suppose two people are watching a sporting match: One has a definite preference for one of the competing teams; the other is more a fan of the sport. Happiness is what the first person feels when his or her team wins or scores; inner harmony is what the second person enjoys throughout the match, regardless the result.

16. The Outcome

What Can We Expect?

When does our inner harmony bloom? Does it come slowly or suddenly? Inner harmony is the last step of the sequence that has been covered in detail throughout this book:

1. We must meditate, intensively and persistently, to develop our faculty of awareness.

2. We should stay permanently mindful during our alert hours to keep harmful mental formations—cravings, aversions, biased views—at bay.

3. Once we control all cravings, aversions and biased views, our anxiety-and-stress terminates.

4. When suffering ends, inner harmony flourishes; whenever anxiety-and-stress returns, inner harmony fades.

In term of results, the critical factor of this whole process is mindfulness, the second step. Our level of mindfulness—how aware and for how long are we able to stay—controls the timing and speed for us to liberate from suffering and let inner harmony enter our lives. If we are unable to stay mindful, harmful formations—our redundant ego—rule our life and set our level of suffering.

Our inability to exercise mindfulness has the support of meditation as a fortunate, correcting resource. If we have difficulties to stay mindful, as almost everybody does, we should practice meditation, the first step of the sequence. The more scattered and distracted our mind, the more we need to meditate. In terms of resolve, meditation overrides mindfulness as the critical factor. Meditation is the only step of the four that demands the allocation of specific time and, indeed, substantial time. The other three factors run in parallel or happen during our daily activities.

Now we can answer the question that titles this section. Our expectations of liberation from anxiety-and-stress—with the consequent appearance of inner harmony—depend totally on our commitment to meditate. After mastering mindfulness, the third and fourth steps will come very smoothly or, more precisely, automatically.

Some teachers, as Indian philosopher Krishnamurti, claim that awareness is easy and natural. That is not so. Mindfulness becomes effortless only after many long hours and days of meditation. The longer we meditate, the sooner our anxiety-and-stress will end; we must not give up. We cannot expect miracles; mindfulness is not a matter of faith and there is no shortcut to this path... Unless we are some sort of Krishnamurti.

There is some good news, however. Moderate dedication to meditation leads to moderate advancements. We may experience some modest but noticeable improvements in our awareness of cravings, aversions and biased views, as well as some reduction in our levels of anxiety-and-stress. We must pay attention to these progresses; all the benefits of meditation materialize—the most notorious are those related with physical and mental health—in proportion to the intensity of our practices.

The best that can happen to us (and it will happen to all those who persevere) is that these progresses boost our determination to spend more hours meditating which will lead to a virtuous circle. As we cut off more and more harmful mental formations, our redundant ego becomes smaller and smaller, anxiety-and-stress decreases, less second arrows hit us, and we experience longer and longer periods of inner harmony. At some point, the redundant ego vanishes and our essential self takes over. Then, after an undefined period, we are mindful most of the time, suffering ends and inner harmony becomes our permanent state.

After Second Arrows End

The Buddha compares his teachings with an improvised structure that a man uses to cross a large stretch of water.[88]

He needs to be soon on the other side, and there are no ferryboats or bridges in the vicinity. As his only option, the traveler collects sticks, branches and creepers from the nearby forest, and puts them together to improvise a raft, which he soon completes with much diligence.

After crossing the river, the man wonders whether he might need the raft later and considers taking it on his shoulders. "What a foolish idea!"—he rethinks—and keeps walking toward his destination.

The Buddha says that his teachings are like the raft of the story. Once *on the other side,* the teachings, as the raft, become useless; we may well abandon them. The theory behind the reality of suffering, its origins and its cessation as well as the directions to follow the path toward the liberation from second arrows (the instructions to meditate, the knowledge of mindfulness's hindrances, favoring factors, benefits, dangers...) are the raft. Travelers of the path must build their own rafts and cross the river. After that, they only need to keep walking.

The steps to put sticks, branches and creepers together are the instructions to meditate; crossing the river is beginning to meditate and making a habit out of it; mindfulness is the continued walk; and the constant practice of meditation is the exercise that keeps us fit for the long journey.

We will not need further instructions when we are on the other side; never again will we need boats or bridges of any kind. Once we have eliminated our redundant ego, the essential self will take over our life. Then effortlessly, without any struggle to complete some goal or reach a certain destination, we will flow spontaneously with our existence. We must keep in mind that we cannot flow on purpose.

Michelangelo, the great Italian Renaissance artist, believed that images already existed in the blocks of marble as if they were locked in there. Before the first cut, he thought, the sculptor should discover the idea within and then proceed to remove the excess material. Michelangelo, so easy for him, just chipped away from the marble what was not statue.

In the same manner, our inflated self, jam-packed with harmful formations, is like a huge stone, very, very heavy; our essential self, our own piece of art, lies somewhere within that rock. If we are to find it, as the artist suggests for marble, we also have to remove the excess. We do possess the skills to chip away the portion that is not really us; the endeavor—just ask Michelangelo—does require much work and perseverance. When we are done, we will experience our own existence and everything else very differently.

Our essential self comes out spontaneously after silencing our mental formations and removing our redundant ego. We do not find our essential self through reasoning dissections or belief systems because these depend upon the mental formations that already make up our inflated self.

We cannot depend upon masters, spiritual teachers or gurus. Some sages might point us in the right direction but nobody can steer us toward our essential self; we have to find it by ourselves. We do not develop, build or refine our inner nature; it is already in there. Neither can we come across it through intellectual gimmicks; the process, as this book has discussed it extensively, is about quieting mental noises and unlearning—de-programming, erasing—harmful mental habits.

Once Michelangelo removed the superfluous fragments in the blocks of marble, the harmony of his *Pietà*, his *David* or his *Moses* was magnificent. When we cut down the surplus material of our inflated self's big stone—our redundant ego, right there, within us, our essential self, with no trace of second arrows, will manifest, vibrating in inner harmony. We just have to remove the unnecessary.

Appendixes

Appendix 1 – Glossary

absorption or meditative states (*jhana* in Pali): Four progressively deeper meditative states that meditators spontaneously experience after patient and persistent practice.

aggregates of personality (*khandha* in Pali): The collection of physical, mental and behavioral qualities that provide us with the sense of being individuals. The aggregates are the five manifestations of our personality, namely, body, sensory signals, perceptions, mental formations and cognition.

anchors: Objects or devices on which meditators focus their attention during their practice. The two most commonly used anchors in mindfulness meditation are our breath and our sensations.

anxiety-and-stress or suffering (*dukkha* in Pali): The set of negative feelings generated by cravings for what we lack (food in excess, friends, love, sex, money, power, prestige, etc.) and aversions to what imaginarily or actually surrounds us (threats, unpleasant people, events or things).

aversion: A feeling of strong dislike or repugnance toward certain people or things with a keen desire to avoid or turn away from them.

appetite: Natural desire, such as the desire for food or sex, necessary to keep up organic life and preserve species; the survival driver to meet biological needs.

biased views: A biased belief, bigoted view or prejudice that lacks backing from positive knowledge. See *opinion*.

body: The totality of parts and inner components of the human body; the body is the first aggregate of personality. The word *body* in some sentences, such *body and brain*, means *body ex-brain*.

Buddha, the: Siddhattha Gotama, the founder of Buddhism.

171

characteristics of human existence: Facts about the nature of human existence; these characteristics are three: impermanence, materiality and suffering (more precisely, the human predisposition to suffering).

cognition (*viññana* in Pali, fifth aggregate of personality): The process of knowing, learning, judging and being aware—our ability to call and use our knowledge, skills and memories—which can only be accessed by ourselves; it is the storehouse for both our library of everything we know, believe and are, and the manual of instructions for everything we can do.

craving: An intense, abnormal desire or longing.

delusion: A persistent false belief held as true despite indisputable evidence to the contrary.

ego (*atta* in Pali): Sense of identity. Since the word *ego* bears a contrasting connotation, this book uses it linked to the adjective *redundant* (see *redundant ego*), not as a synonym of *self*.

emotion: Body's reactions to certain external or internal stimuli (e.g., a threat or a remembrance).

essential self: The reduced or downsized self when the harmful formations have been silenced; what is left of our inflated self when we suppress the redundant portion.

favoring factors: Favoring factors are the conditions that help us to surmount the hindrances to meditation and mindfulness. The Buddha suggests seven favoring factors: attention to cravings and aversions, calm (both physical and mental), silence, equanimity, determination, learning and joy.

fear: Natural apprehension caused by anticipation or awareness of danger, the survival driver to manage threats.

feeling: The perception of emotional reactions, that is, the recording and processing the brain makes when it becomes aware of such reactions.

foundations of mindfulness: The domains or objects on which we should maintain our attention to gain freedom from anxiety-and-stress.

hindrances: Hindrances to meditation and mindfulness are the conditions that prevent or discourage us from practicing meditation or mindfulness. The Buddha suggests five culprits: greed, hostility, sloth, restlessness and doubt.

impermanence (*annica* in Pali, one of the characteristics of human existence): The permanent changing nature of everything.

inner harmony (*nibbana* in Pali): The experience of the total, unconditional cessation of suffering; the state of being at peace even in the face of difficulties.

level zero: The mental state meditators reach when they abide the basic definition of mindfulness meditation for a reasonably long period (say, for example, forty-five minutes to an hour).

levels 1 through 4: The four absorptions or meditative states of deep meditation.

materiality (*annatta* in Pali, one of the characteristics of human existence): The physical or worldly nature of human life according to which our self is the result of some neuronal software that originates in and operates from our brain, and manifests through our body. Materiality implies the absence or lack in human existence of any entity that could be regarded as an immaterial self or an immaterial essence within, behind or parallel to the physical entity. Literally, the Pali word means *lack of soul or self*; suggested alternative translations include *impersonality* and *nothingness*.

meditation: The broad set of physical and mental exercises through which their practitioners manage and control their attention in search of certain benefits such as stress reduction, health improvement, spiritual growth or performance enhancement.

meditative states: See *absorptions*.

mental formations (*sankhara* in Pali, fourth aggregate of personality): The behavioral routines—physical or mental—that we learn voluntarily or acquire unwillingly.

mind: The workings of the brain that are exclusive of human beings; the activities performed by the human brain and that are not performed by the brain of the other mammals which posses a similar organ.

mindfulness (*khandha* in Pali): The permanent awareness of life as it unfolds. More specifically, mindfulness is (1) the active awareness of whatever we are doing, and (2) the passive, nonjudgmental awareness of our body, our sensations and our mental states.

mindfulness meditation: A mental exercise during which meditators with their eyes gently closed, sitting in a comfortable position and in a quiet environment, adopt a passive attitude, and focus attention on certain anchors in order to enhance their daily awareness; whenever meditators notice that their attention is off-course, they take it back to the anchor of their choice.

opinion: A belief or judgment stronger than an impression but not strong enough for certainty.

Pali Canon: A voluminous collection of documents that contains, among many other texts, the discourses of the Buddha.

pain: Distressing sensation that results from events, such as aches, injuries and other physical disarrays that negatively affect the body of animals.

perceptions (*khandha* in Pali, third aggregate of personality): The interpretation the brain makes of sensory signals.

phenomenon: Any perceptible event.

physical individuality: The body.

redundant ego: The share of self, programmed in our brain by harmful mental formations, that is discretionary and, therefore, it can be *disconnected* or *turned off.* Each person's redundant ego is the seat of his or her suffering.

self (*atta* in Pali): Sense of identity or symbolic identity that manifests as continuity and consistency in a person's behavior. The self is a super-complex piece of neuronal software that performs its work through the brain, the seat of our mind.

sensations: The consolidated sensory phenomenon, this is, the merging of sensory signals (that occur throughout the whole body) and perception (that occur in the brain).

sensory signals (*vedana* in Pali, second aggregate of personality): Bodily reactions to external or inner stimuli.

suffering or anxiety-and-stress (*dukkha* in Pali): The set of negative feelings generated by cravings for what we lack (food in excess, friends, love, sex, money, power, prestige, etc.) and aversions to what imaginarily or actually surrounds us (threats, unpleasant people, events or things).

symbolic identity: The mental identity—the self—as opposed to the physical individuality; the neuronal software that controls the body.

teachings (*dhamma* in Pali): The essence of the Buddha's doctrine, which leaves out the myths and the religious portion of Buddhism. The word *teachings* is one of the English translations of the Pali word *dhamma,* the most important word in Buddhist literature. Other translations include *law, natural law* and *doctrine.*

Appendix 2 – The Foundations of Mindfulness

Guidelines for Meditation and Mindfulness

The discourses about the foundations of mindfulness, both the short[89] and the long[90] versions, are two of the most widely read and studied Buddhist texts. Body, sensations, mental states and the essence of the Buddha's teachings are the four foundations of mindfulness. Each discourse consists of four sections, one for each foundation.

There are four sets of guidelines or descriptions in this appendix. The first two, on breath (a function of the body) and sensations, contain the actual instructions for meditation.[91] The third one describes the practice of mindfulness around mental states, during our alert hours; mental states are not common anchors to practice meditation.

The fourth item corresponds to the description of what the Buddha refers to as "right concentration." The Sage's description corresponds to the second stage, levels one to four, of the practice of mindfulness meditation and is along the line of what was presented in the section "Flow of Sensations" in Chapter 15. The fourth section of the short version of the discourse contains the essence of the Buddha's teachings, which are the five notions that the Buddha wants us to understand, not intellectually but experientially, as part of our traveling toward the cessation of second arrows. The five notions are the hindrances, the aggregates of personality, the internal and external sense-spheres,[92] the favoring factors and the four truths. Throughout this book, either in its main part or as endnotes, these five areas are covered.

The directions for focusing attention on the breath (first item) or sensations (second item) as presented here are not the typical instructions that meditation teachers commonly speak or read in their classes. Instead, they illustrate what should be happening in the body and the mind of meditators while they are sitting in meditation. This wording reflects, in this author's interpretation, the Buddha's intention to motivate students to *fly solo,* instead of providing them with the *standard* line-by-line instructions.

For example, the sentences below do not contain commands such as "focus attention on your breath, inhale a long breath, exhale a long breath, etc." Instead, the Buddha says, "breathing in a long breath, the meditator knows, 'the meditator is breathing in a long breath.' " The directions for "Mindfulness of Mental States" (third item) and "Meditation beyond Anchors" (fourth item) follow a similar pattern.

The challenge of meditation teachers, when directing their classes, is to convert the descriptions below into not-distracting, general guidelines. The attention of every student will always be focused on different things and, while some are inhaling, other might be exhaling or holding their respiration. When students gain sufficient experience, they should be able to meditate without the need of any voice directing their practice. The challenge of the meditation students is to maintain a sharp and nonjudgmental attention at every moment.

Meditation Focused on the Breath

And how does a meditator[93] remain focused on the body as just the body? Herein, having gone to the forest, to the shade of a tree, or to an empty place, a meditator sits down with legs crossed, keeps the body erect, and directs attention to the breath. Always mindful, the meditator breathes in; always mindful, the meditator breathes out.

Breathing in a long breath, the meditator knows, "the meditator is breathing in a long breath." Breathing out a long breath, the meditator knows, "the meditator is breathing out a long breath." Breathing in a short breath, the meditator knows, "the meditator is breathing in a short breath." Breathing out a short breath, the meditator knows, "the meditator is breathing out a short breath."

Experiencing the whole body, the meditator will breathe in, thus training his/her faculty of awareness. Experiencing the whole body, the meditator will breathe out, thus training his/her faculty of awareness. Letting the process of breathing calm (without exerting any conscious control over it), the meditator will breathe in, thus training his/her faculty of awareness. Letting the process of breathing calm (without exerting any conscious control over it), the meditator will breathe out, thus training his/her faculty of awareness.

In this way, the meditator remains focused, both internally and externally, on the body as just a body (not his/hers, not a physical individuality, not a symbolic identity, just an impermanent phenomenon), just a body that is being experienced. The meditator's mindfulness that "there is a body" is established to the extent necessary for bare knowledge and remembrance. And the meditator remains detached and clings to nothing in the world.

This is how a meditator remains focused on the body as a body.

Meditation Focused on Sensations

And how does a meditator remain focused on sensations as just sensations? Herein, when experiencing a pleasant sensation, a meditator knows, "the meditator is experiencing a pleasant sensation"; when experiencing a painful sensation, he/she knows, "the meditator is experiencing a painful sensation"; when experiencing a neutral sensation, he/she knows, "the meditator is experiencing a neutral sensation."

When experiencing a gross pleasant sensation, he/she knows, "the meditator is experiencing a gross pleasant sensation."

When experiencing a subtle pleasant sensation, he/she knows...

When experiencing a gross unpleasant sensation, he/she knows...

When experiencing a subtle unpleasant sensation, he/she knows...

When experiencing a gross neutral sensation, he/she knows...

When experiencing a subtle neutral sensation, he/she knows...

In this way, the meditator remains focused, both internally and externally, on sensations as sensations (not his/hers, not a physical individuality, not a symbolic identity, but just an impermanent phenomenon), just sensations that are being experienced. The meditator's mindfulness that "there are sensations" is established to the extent necessary for bare knowledge and remembrance. And the meditator remains detached and clings to nothing in the world.

This is how a meditator remains focused on sensations as just sensations.

Mindfulness of Mental States

And how does a person who is mindful continue to perceive, again and again, mental states as just mental states?

Desires or greed:[94] Herein, when a person who is mindful perceives his/her cravings, that person knows, "This is a mind with cravings"; when a person who is mindful does not perceive any cravings, that person knows, "This is a mind without cravings."

Fears or hatred: When a mindful person perceives his/her aversions, the mindful person knows, "This is a mind with aversions"; when a mindful person does not perceive any aversions, the mindful person knows, "This is a mind without aversions."

Delusion: When a mindful person perceives his/her biased views, the mindful person knows, "This is a mind with biased views"; when a mindful person does not perceive any biased opinion, the mindful person knows, "This is a mind without biased opinions."

Lethargy: When a mindful person perceives he/she is lethargic, the mindful person knows, "This is a mind with lethargy"; when a mindful person perceives he/she is hyperactive, the mindful person knows, "This is a mind with hyperactivity."

Openness: When a mindful person perceives he/she is open-minded, the mindful person knows, "This is a mind with openness"; when a mindful person perceives he/she is narrow-minded, the mindful person knows, "This is a mind with restraints."

Realization: When a mindful person perceives that there may be mental states higher than the current one, the mindful person knows, "There may be mental states higher than the current one"; when a mindful person perceives that there may not be mental states higher than the current one, the mindful person knows, "There may not be mental states higher than the current one."

Concentration: When a mindful person perceives he/she is concentrated, the mindful person knows, "This is a mind with concentration"; when a mindful person perceives he/she is scattered, the mindful person knows, "This is a mind that is scattered."

Freedom: When a mindful person perceives he/she is free, the mindful person knows, "This is a free mind"; when a mindful person perceives he/she has attachments, the mindful person knows, "This is a mind with attachments."

In this way, the mindful person dwells perceiving, both internally and externally, mental states as mental states (not his/hers, not a physical individuality, not a symbolic identity, but just an impermanent phenomenon), just mental states that are being experienced. The meditator's mindfulness that "there are mental states" is established to the extent necessary for bare knowledge and remembrance. And the mindful person remains detached and clings to nothing in the world.

This is how a meditator dwells perceiving mental states as just mental states.

Meditation beyond Anchors

And what, meditators, is right concentration?[95] When meditators let go greed, hostility, restlessness, sloth and doubt (the hindrances to meditation and mindfulness), they enter the first meditative state, a state of subtle but real joy, born from physical isolation, accompanied by directed thought (focusing on breath) and discursive thinking (observation of sensations).

With the subsiding of directed thought and discursive thinking, meditators enter a second meditative state, a state of joy as well as physical and mental calm, born from mental isolation, free from directed thought and discursive thinking.

When meditators become indifferent to the joy they are experiencing, remaining imperturbable, mindful and clearly aware, they enter a third state of meditation, a state of equanimity and impartial calm, and stay fully conscious and lucid of this equanimity (born of the suspension of all relations with both the sensible world and with memory).

When meditators, sharply attentive but neutral to any sensation or feeling they may be perceiving, detached from both joy or the absence of joy, meditators enter a fourth state, an even deeper state of pure awareness born of equanimity.

This, meditators, is called right concentration.

Appendix 3 – The Physiology of Meditation

Neurology Basics and Summary

Neurons are the cells of our nervous system which process and send out electrochemical signals. Neurotransmitters are chemicals that neurons use to send instructions to a neighbor neuron. Neuronal connections, or synapses, are the junctions through which source neurons send neurotransmitters to target cells. Chemical receptors are large molecules in target neurons that recognize neurotransmitters and interpret the instructions from the source neuron.

Neuronal connections are either excitatory, when the nerve signal increases the firing activity of the receiving cell, or inhibitory, the opposite, when the signal reduces the firing activity of the receiving cell.

There are many types of neurotransmitters; dopamine, serotonin, acetylcholine, glutamate (a salt of glutamic acid) and GABA (gamma-amino butyric acid) are some of the best known. Glutamate most often produces excitatory results; GABA commonly displays inhibitory characteristics. Most neurons release either glutamate (excitatory effects) or GABA (inhibitory effects).

The excitatory-inhibitory consequence of a signal upon the target neuron depends on both the neurotransmitter sent by the source neuron and the type of chemical receptor receiving the neurotransmitter in the target neuron.

The expressions *excitatory neuron* and *inhibitory neuron,* which this book uses sometimes, are simplified references to neurons that release glutamate and GABA respectively rather than absolute distinctions. Since there are several players participating in every transmission—source neurons, synapses, neurotransmitters, chemical receptors in the target neuron—the expressions *inhibitory mechanisms* (or *inhibitory circuits*) and *excitatory mechanisms* (or *excitatory cir-*

182

cuits), are used to cover the whole activating or restraining processes. The core interest of this appendix is in inhibitory mechanisms.

Mindfulness meditation is an intensive workout of our neuronal inhibitory mechanisms; such workouts keep these mechanisms in good shape or restore their functional capacity when it deteriorates.

We do not see our inhibitory circuits alternating between on and off positions, not even with the sophisticated imaging tools available these days; this technology displays neuronal activity but cannot tell whether that activity is inhibitory or excitatory. Meditation, however, leads to other measurable effects of restraining *commands*. Such effects, which are common to all forms of meditation, include a decrease in heart rate, a reduction in breathing frequency, a decline in oxygen consumption, and a slower metabolic rate.

Workout of Inhibitory Mechanisms

Every task we perform involves the intervention of both excitatory and inhibitory neurons. In physical exercises, such as dancing or ball juggling, which necessarily include mental activity, the neuronal work in the whole nervous system is both excitatory and inhibitory. In purely mental activities, such as chess or Sudoku, the neuronal activity, which takes place mostly in the brain, involves much more excitatory than inhibitory activity. Nevertheless, the role of inhibition is extremely important in both situations.

How do we specifically train our inhibitory mechanisms? Since we cannot witness what is not happening, how do we keep fit such mechanisms whose work—stopping or slowing down actions—is invisible? This is exactly what the practice of mindfulness meditation does. In general, most forms of meditation are good trainers of inhibitory mechanisms; mindfulness meditation, however, is the most effective.

Mindfulness meditation, as we said, is the practice of directed mindfulness to make it a permanent habit. While meditating we discontinue or slow down physical and mental activity, which means that we turn on—we activate—all the silencing inhibitory army that sends stop and tone down instructions to the excitatory circuits that control motor, visual, acoustic, olfactory, tasting and mental tasks.

Mindfulness meditation is the *purposeful* stopping or slowing of our alert state functions. What happens to our neurons while we meditate? When we start a meditation session, we go through a wide variety of sensory and perceptual experiences, which originate from the continuous activation and deactivation of inhibitory circuits.

As we enter deeper levels of introspection, we isolate ourselves not only from external sensory signals (that is the easy part) but also from our incessant mental wandering. As physical and mental passivity *peak* and inaction *prevails,* millions of inhibitory connections turn on, block distracting thoughts, and make meditators undergo some singular sensory experiences. These experiences change from person to person and even from session to session for the same meditator. Still, as any other mental event, such experiences are the product of neuronal activity and not, by any means, of *metaphysical* phenomena.

Though there may be many variations in mindfulness meditation routines, the sequence below is typical and contains sufficient information to explain the association between mindfulness meditation and neuronal inhibition. While beginners normally stay within the first four or five numerals of this progression, persistent meditators regularly reach and experience the deeper introspection levels. The sequence is as follows:

1. Just by sitting still, quiet, with eyes closed and in an isolated place, an important fraction of our excitatory circuits—the motors, the talkers, the observers, the

listeners and, if we have not eaten anything during the previous hours, the digesters—goes to rest. All the associated inhibitory neurons stay on. Thus far, except for posture and consciousness, meditating and sleeping are similar activities.

2. When we become aware of gross sensations—our clothes, the contact with our seat or the floor—the inhibitory connections that ordinarily block such sensations are turned off (we perceive such sensations; sensations are on).

3. When we focus attention onto the flow of our breath, inhibitory mechanisms turn on to shut off distractions.

4. As distractions interfere, inhibitory mechanisms turn off to let distracting thoughts enter (involuntarily). When we notice we are distracted, we go back to Item 4 (inhibitory mechanisms turn on again).

5. With practice and patience, we are able to maintain our awareness on our breath for longer and longer periods. When this happens, subtle sensations appear in different parts of our body, which implies that inhibitory circuits, both at the central and peripheral systems, are turned off (sensations are on) to allow perception of those sensory signals.

6. As new sensations appear (as more inhibitory connections turn off), we move our attention to wherever we perceive a new sensation: Attention follows sensations.

7. We may also scan our body and focus attention on *silent* locations; after a few seconds, a new subtle sensation shows up (some inhibitory connections turn off) right there where we perceived nothing an instant ago: Subtle sensations follow attention. (We just move attention to a different place when no sensation appears in a particular location.)

8. With continued practice, we will perceive throughout the whole body a very pleasant flow of subtle sensa-

tions that we observe with sharp attention. New sensory signals we perceive are inhibitory neurons that are turning off; new active sensations that disappear are inhibitory neurons that turn on.

9. When distractions take over, attention goes back to our breath; some inhibitory connections turn on to shut off distractions. And so on.

The role of inhibitory mechanisms is similar to that of guards at private premises or porters in public events. When they are on duty—that is, exercising their vigilant obligation—only authorized people enter, as it should be. When they are not exercising their duties—that is, absent or inattentive—anybody can enter and disturb common operations. Similarly, when our inhibitory custodians are off duty, intruding and disrupting thoughts—cravings and aversions, addictions and phobias—take over our mind.

Mindfulness meditation retrains inhibitory mechanisms in their guarding roles: Who can enter our mind? What functions can they request from excitatory neurons? How much of each duty do they authorize? When should the excitatory circuits shut off?

From Order to Disarray and Back to Order

In our remote ancestors, pleasure and pain were survival mechanisms designed through natural selection. By generating the desires that call for the repetition of specific beneficial actions, both physiological and social, pleasure became a survival advantage for individuals and species. Similarly, the experience of pain led to fears that set off automatic alarms when threatening dangers emerged; the timely fight-or-flight conditioned response was instrumental for survival.

Our desires and fears, therefore, are natural reactions, which our genetic code programs as neuronal circuits in our brain; attentive inhibitory mechanisms, however, should stop such

186

responses once the demanding need or the threatening danger is satisfied or controlled.

Unfortunately, our reactions to needs and threats sometimes go in the wrong direction. The frequent repetition of an event or the high impact of a single episode might alter inhibitory mechanisms; they fail then to block the conditioned neuronal circuits that urgently demand repetition or avoidance. If after the satisfaction of a particular need, the neural patterns of desires stay on, the temporary wants progressively become cravings, addictions, or even compulsive demands. Similarly, if after the disappearance of a threat the neural patterns of fears remain active, the transitory worries become aversions, phobias, or even out-of-control panics, hatred or rage.

Anxiety-and-stress begins with cravings and aversions. This is when mindfulness and mindfulness meditation prove most effective, and with their dutiful practice, we can confidently get things back to normal. Unfortunately, during this cravings and aversions stage, it is also when we deny or tolerate suffering: Social drinks and classy distastes are widely accepted.

When inhibitory mechanisms go wild and unruly, the simple thought of the conditioning events triggers cravings for repeating pleasure and dreads for avoiding pain. Either in the addictive or in the repulsive direction, the whole process becomes an unbearable treadmill; then, misbehaviors that are more complex arise and our anxiety-and-stress becomes apparent to others.

Cognitive sciences are finding that many disarrays, such as substance abuse, bulimia, sexual addictions, obsessive-compulsive disorders and post-traumatic stress disorders, have roots in the malfunctioning of inhibitory mechanisms. At this point, specialized psychological or psychiatric assistance becomes necessary. Many therapists are now using mindfulness meditation with their patients in parallel with other treatments.

INNER HARMONY

Mindfulness meditation, the intensive exercise of large groups of inhibitory neurons, helps to bring back inhibitory processes to order and harmony. It is both a preventive, quite advisable approach for everybody—cravings and aversion are always ready to attack—and the most effective corrective prescription to control anxiety-and-stress.

Appendix 4 – Meditation's Quick Reference Guide

This appendix is a quick reference guide for mindfulness meditation and contains everything students need to remember to become serious meditators—they might well forget all said so far about both the wisdom of the teachings of the Buddha and the insights of evolutionary psychology. Such knowledge, however interesting, is not necessary to sit in meditation.

Stages: There are two stages in mindfulness meditation. In the first one, active attention (level zero), students maintain their attention focused on the anchors of their preference. In the second stage, passive awareness (levels 1 through 4), meditators surrender to the meditation experience. Figuratively speaking, in the first stage practitioners sit to meditate; in the second one, *meditation happens to practitioners*. The tables at the end of this appendix provide an overall picture of the sequence to follow in the meditation process.

Active attention: The first stage has five options (1 through 5), starting with the observation of the breath, the entry point, or option 1. Beginners might want to spend several meditation sessions in each option before trying the next one and move up progressively; they do not need to go through the five choices and they might even stay forever in option 1 if they feel comfortable with it. Experienced meditators may use these five broad guidelines indistinctly in their practices. Beginning every session at option 1 is advisable but not required. The sequence upwards (options 2 through 5) is arbitrary and meditators do not need to follow it in any particular order; they may change it from session to session, skip options if they develop some preferences, or spend the whole session in just one anchor. The voice of a teacher or a set of pre-recorded instructions are indeed helpful during the active attention stage.

Observation of the breath (option 1): Meditators focus attention on their breath and remain aware of the flow of air—

whether it is entering or leaving the nostrils, whether it is slow or fast, steady or irregular, deep or shallow—with neither judgment of what is going on nor intention to alter its natural flow. When their mind wanders and students notice they are distracted, they simply return their attention to their breath, with no thoughts about why or how he or she became distracted.

The observation of the breath, the universal anchor, is:

1. the starting point for beginners when they sit to meditate not only for the very first time, but also during all their early sessions (when meditation is not yet a habit);

2. a suitable entry point (though not a must) for every meditation session;

3. the best technique to pull attention back when digressions have the mind flying;

4. a practical approach that may be used (and many meditators do so) as the only technique.

Observation of the body's parts (option 2): Meditators might begin their practice with attention centered on their breath. After a short while, they change the starting anchor and begin rotating their attention throughout their whole body. Then they *scan* the different parts of their *external* body (fingers, hands, elbows, mouth, tongue...) in any sequence they choose. Students should hold attention at every place for a few seconds and then move the focus of their attention to a new one. There are no rules about the sequence to follow but it is important that every part of the body be visited once in every cycle. Depending upon the time assigned, there might be one or several scanning cycles in a session. When distractions arise, students simply return attention to the body part where they lost track of the practice or start over a new cycle; they might also want to focus attention on their breath before reinitiating the new cycle.

Observation of sensations in the area right below the nostrils (option 3): This option introduces sensations in the meditation experience (options 1 and 2 were about the body). Meditators should focus their attention on sensations in the small area between the nostrils and the upper lip. Sensations to observe are, in general, very subtle—it may take a while before meditators perceive them; they might be sensations of any kind—dryness, wetness, heat, cold, tickling, flow of air, tickling, itching, etc. Meditators must not judge those sensations, just be aware of them. If students do not feel any sensation at the area right below the nostrils, they should simply acknowledge the absence of sensations and keep the attention on this little place, for the whole meditation session, if necessary. With perseverance, sensations will eventually show up and students are to maintain their impartial attention on such sensations or on the area where they are supposed to manifest until the end of the practice.

Scanning the body for pleasant, unpleasant or neutral sensations (option 4): In option 4, meditators are to scan their bodies to become aware at each part of either the presence of pleasant, unpleasant or neutral sensations, or the absence of any sensation (when there is none). This option is similar to option 2 but this time students are to watch the sensations perceived at every part of the body and impartially observe whether they are pleasant, unpleasant or neutral.

Scanning the body in search of gross or subtle sensations (option 5): Option 5 is similar to option 4. This time, however, meditators become aware of the subtlety or the grossness of their sensations (rather than the pleasantness, disagreeableness or neutrality of sensations). Students are also to be aware of the absence of sensations when there is none.

Passive awareness: Levels 1 to 4 make up the stage of passive awareness. The transit from the stage of active attention to this stage and from each of its levels to the next one is to be spontaneous. Students should not worry if they do not enter any of these levels and must not strive to be there.

191

Options in Stage 1 Mindfulness Meditation

Levels & Options	Stages	Anchors	Overall Guideline	When Distractions Arise...
Option 1	Stage 1: Active attention (Level zero)	Breath	Observation of the breath	...Return attention to the breath.
Option 2		Body	Scanning the body in a sequence and becoming conscious of every part	
Option 3		Sensations on one single spot	Focusing on sensations in the area between the nostrils and the upper lip	
Option 4		Sensations throughout the body	Scanning the body in a sequence and becoming aware at each part of either the presence of pleasant, unpleasant or neutral sensations, or the absence of any sensation (when there is none)	
Option 5		Sensations throughout the body	Scanning the body in a sequence while observing at each part the gross or subtle sensations that are present, or becoming aware of the absence of sensations (when there are none)	

Appendixes

Meditative States in Stage 2 of Mindfulness Meditation

Levels & Options	Stages	Meditative States	Overall Guideline	When Distractions Arise...
Level 1	Stage 2: Passive awareness (Levels 1 through 4)	Joy	Scanning the body in no sequence and observing (mostly) subtle sensations	...Return attention to the breath.
Level 2		Calm	Observing the spontaneous flow of (mostly) subtle sensations	
Level 3		Equanimity	Staying fully conscious and lucid of the experienced equanimity	
Level 4		Pure awareness	Being present in the silence of the mind	

Throughout this book, mindfulness meditation has been explained with the simplicity that should characterize its practice. Still the Buddhist or evolutionary terminology used to back the rationale of meditation might have created in some readers a false image of complexity. This misunderstanding might have discouraged some potential meditators.

Meditation, from the perspective of its instructions, is very simple; the brevity of this appendix confirms this simplicity. This Quick Reference Guide is this book's last try to convince readers to undertake meditation. Meditation has little to do with theory; only the direct experience of the results of meditation will show students the incontrovertible beauty of inner harmony.

Acknowledgments

A very special organization and several people contributed importantly to the completion of this book; they, directly or circumstantially, provided their support in a variety of ways. Some came voluntarily, a thoughtful assistance that was especially encouraging when my hesitation on this writing project was peaking. The support from others was so subtle that the contributors did not even know they were helping. A few more were the crucial and invaluable talents that most writers require from editors and designers. I am grateful to all of them.

Up front, I want to offer my deepest appreciation to the Vipassana Meditation Centers for the opportunity that I have had over the last seven years to participate in their training programs. Although I had practiced meditation long before my attendance at my first ten-day retreat and in spite of some minor divergences with their approach, the Vipassana techniques allowed me to live and learn firsthand the subtleties of mindfulness meditation.

My direct experience of deep meditation states, the absence of ceremonial ornaments or images in the Vipassana centers, and the removal of any dogmatic content from their lectures and instructions allowed me to understand intimately something that I already knew through reasoning. The practice of mindfulness meditation relates in no way with any religion or belief system, and excludes sectarian affiliations of any kind.

Second, I want to thank psychologist Dr. Cheryl Browne for reviewing my manuscripts and making valuable comments at different stages of the project. Making the experience of inner harmony the book's core subject removes the phantom of negativity that some people wrongly see in the teachings of the Buddha (as a consequence of the word *suffering*). This was one of Cheryl's several specific recommendations.

195

I am also indebted to neuroscientist Jason Shumake. Dr. Shumake and Cheryl spent many hours reviewing my reasoning on why mindfulness meditation is helpful in the lessening of harmful mental formations. Though my theory that mindfulness meditation is an intensive exercise of inhibitory circuits still needs to be tested, Dr. Shumake considers it plausible. His observations mean a lot to me.

Fourth, I thank Jo'son Bell, a teacher of the Vipassana Group, for his friendship and counsel, and for his hospitality in dozens of meditation sittings in his home. If I believed in fate (which I do not), I would say that destiny put him in my path six years ago when he moved to Smyrna, Georgia, to a house less than a mile away from my home. Through Jo'son, I met Daniel Gómez, another Vipassana teacher, who had read my book in Spanish *Hacia el Buda desde el occidente* (*Toward the Buddha from the West*). His insistence to translate *Hacia el Buda* into English has been a driver in my enthusiasm to complete *Inner Harmony*. I thank Daniel for his friendly pressure and continued encouragement.

Next, I want to express my thanks to Dr. Akiyoshi Kitaoka, Department of Psychology, Ritsumeikan University, in Kyoto, Japan, for granting me his permission to use *Morning Sunlight*, the beautiful design on the cover of this book. I could not think of a better illustration of inner harmony. Finally, I thank Madeline Hopkins for her thoughtful and meticulous editing, and for the excellent work polishing my English sentences and correcting the mistakes most authors make when they write in a second language.

Notes and Bibliographical References

The following "Notes and Bibliographical References" contain a blend of numerous comments and source references as well as an alphabetic list of all the authors, scholars and religious figures quoted or mentioned in this book. [96] The "Notes" are extensions of the core subject of the book that are not critical by any means for its overall understanding; they simply provide further information on cognitive sciences, Buddhism and Eastern thought.

The "Bibliographical References" are the list of publications (books, magazines and websites) that support this work, or from which literal or adapted quotations have been taken.

The word *adapted* demands some clarification because it refers to passages of the Buddha's discourses, which were originally written (and perhaps pronounced) in Pali language. The author's knowledge of this language is limited to a few Buddhist keywords that are sufficient to capture the challenges Pali scholars must face when translating the Buddha's messages. The English versions of every discourse often come up with different sentences for almost every paragraph, which makes it difficult for the reader to capture a single unambiguous idea. Therefore, the confusing sentences in different versions of the same discourse have been adapted, with much careful judgment, to the context of the book.

The following list includes the main sources (compilations of the Buddha's discourses or words) that have been consulted, starting with the names of the scholars who translated the original texts. The numbered reference of each quote in this book points to the specific text where it appears in the Pali Canon; each quote of the Buddha's words, therefore, might come from one or a combination of several of the following sources:

- Maurice Walshe: *The Long Discourses of the Buddha: A Translation of the Digha Nikaya.* Somerville, Massachusetts: Wisdom Publications, 1995.
- Bhikkhu Ñanamoli: *The Middle Length Discourses of the Buddha – A New Translation of the Majjhima Nikaya.* Translated by Bhikkhu Ñanamoli and Bhikkhu Bodhi. Boston, Massachusetts: Wisdom Publications, 1995.
- Bhikkhu Bodhi: *The Connected Discourses of the Buddha – A Translation of the Samyutta Nikaya.* Somerville, Massachusetts: Wisdom Publications, 2000.
- Analayo: *Satipaṭṭhāna Sutta – The Direct Path of Realization.* Cambridge, Massachusetts: Windhorse Publications, 2003.
- Thanissaro Bhikkhu, Soma Thera and Nyanasatta Thera, translators. *Access to Insight: Readings to Theravada Buddhism. Tipitaka – The Pali Canon.* http://www.accesstoinsight.org/tipitaka/index.html. 2005–2013.
- U Jotika and U Dhamminda, translators. *Mahasatipatthana Sutta: The Great Discourse on Steadfast Mindfulness.* Buddhanet: Buddha Dharma Association Inc. http://www.buddhanet.net/imol/mahasati, retrieved August 29, 2012.
- Ananda Maitreya. *The Dhammapada: The Path of Truth.* Translated by Ananda Maitreya. Berkeley, California: Parallax Press, 1995.
- Byrom, Thomas. *The Dhammapada: The Sayings of the Buddha. A Rendering by Thomas Byrom.* Boston & London: Shambhala Publications, Inc., 1993.
- Easwaran, Eknath. *The Dhammapada: Translated for the Modern Reader by Eknath Easwaran.* Tomales, California: Nilgiri Press, 1985.

Notes and Bibliographical References

¹**The Buddha's teachings and the Pali Canon**: The Buddha's teachings appear in the Pali Canon, the oldest and largest text of the Buddhist scriptures, which consists of three divisions. The Division of Discourses, which contains hundreds of the Buddha's dissertations, is the most important part of the Canon and the only one quoted in this book. The Division of Discourses has five collections or *nikayas*: *Digha Nikaya, Majjhima Nikaya, Samyutta Nikaya, Anguttara Nikaya* and *Khuddaka Nikaya*. References to any one of the Buddha's discourses contain: (1) The collection's name, (2) the index number within the collection, (3) the title of the discourse in Pali and (4) the title of the discourse in English. Most discourses (several translations for some texts) can be located in the Web by searching the first three items. The *Khuddaka Nikaya*, the fifth collection, does not have indexing. However, the two texts of this collection that this book quotes (*Dhammapada: The Path of the Teachings* and *Sutta Nipata*) do have paragraphs' numbers that facilitate the location of the references within the discourse.

² *Khuddaka Nikaya*: *Dhammapada 19-20*: *The Path of the Teachings 19-20*.

³ *Anguttara Nikaya 3.65*: *Kalama Sutta: To the Kalamas*.

⁴ **Buddhist word**: Pali, an Indo-Aryan language of the Prakrit group, is the language of the Pali Canon and, for this reason, this book makes the expression *Buddhist word* equivalent to *Pali word*. The first language of the Buddha probably was Prakrit Magadhi, the language of the ancient kingdom of Magadha in Northeast India. Sanskrit is the second most important language of Buddhism.

⁵ **Glossary:** Appendix 1 contains definitions for specific terminology of Buddhism and psychology as well as for the usage given to some words. For Buddhist terms, this appendix also shows the word in Pali language.

---

[6] *Samyutta Nikaya* 36.6. *Sallatha Sutta: The Arrow.*

[7] **Life is not suffering:** The first truth establishes the reality—the existence—of anxiety-and-stress. This does not mean, however, that life is suffering, as some antagonists of Buddhism claim. This interpretation assigns a pessimistic stance to the teachings of the Sage. Such a position is wrong. According to the Buddha, we face hard situations permanently but it is our choice to take action and manage our mental states. Our capacity to eliminate suffering is what makes it optional. The Buddha did say, "It is difficult to conduct life as a human being," which means that life is unavoidably difficult (*Khuddaka Nikaya: Dhammapada 182: The Path of the Teachings 182.*) When there are troubles, the possibility to suffer is always real. No question about it, suffering is indeed associated with such difficulty.

[8] **The four noble truths:** The four truths, known by all schools of Buddhism as the four noble truths, are the essence of the teachings of the Buddha. *Noble* corresponds to the Pali adjective *aria*, which refers to the Arian (or Indo-European) race, which arrived in India fifteen centuries prior to the Buddha's time. Because *noble* does not add any meaning to the truths, such adjective is not used in this book. The first declaration is the truth of suffering; the second, the truth of the origin of suffering; the third, the truth of inner harmony; and the last one, the path to follow toward the cessation of suffering. The four truths were presented by the Buddha in his first discourse, the text of which is at *Samyutta Nikaya 56.11: Dhammacakkappavattana Sutta: Setting the Wheel of Dhamma in Motion.*

[9] Damasio, Antonio. *The Feeling of What Happens: Body and Emotions in the Making of Consciousness.* New York: Harcourt, Inc., 1999.

[10] Sun Tzu (Griffith, Samuel B., translator): *The Art of War.* Oxford: Oxford University Press, 2005.

[11] **Masochism**: The similarity in the workings of pleasure and pain might also explain the oddity of masochism, an anomaly characterized by the perception of pleasure while being subjected to pain or abuse.

[12] **Mental formations**: Mental formations are one of the most important notions in the teachings of the Buddha. Translations of *sankhara,* the Pali word, include the terms *fabrications, formations, volitional formations* and *mental conditionings.* "*Sankharas* are *co-doings*, things that act in concert with other things, or things that are made by a combination of other things," says Bhikkhu Bodhi, the American Buddhist monk and scholar. (*Anicca Vata Sankhara* by Bhikkhu Bodhi, www.accesstoinsight.org, 2005-2012. Retrieved April 23, 2012.)

[13] **Conditionings and mental formations**: The stimulus-response conditionings (pleasure-craving or pain-aversion) that generate mental formations are often direct and evident (like in gluttony) but they may also be indirect or unclear (as when we dislike the friends of our enemy).

[14] **The origin of suffering**: While keeping the essence of the message, the text of the second truth as presented here contains some extended interpretations that include both cravings and aversions as the origins of anxiety-and-stress. The original discourse of the Buddha, according to several English translations, refers only to cravings. However, aversions appear in several other discourses that imply that cravings and aversions are both at the root of suffering. Furthermore, biased opinions also lead to anxiety-and-stress. Because of the way they function, biased opinions may be assimilated to a certain kind of cravings; this extension makes biased opinions an additional element in the origins of suffering, which they definitely are. This expanded scope of the second truth is not specifically dispelled in its original wording.

[15] Becker, Ernest. *The Denial of Death*. New York: Free Press Paperbags, 1973.

[16] **Pain and brain**: Brain tissues are not sensitive because they lack pain receptors. Headaches come from disruptions of sensory structures around the brain.

[17] **Sense of identity in anthropoid apes**: There is much controversy on whether some animals (such as anthropoid apes, elephants, dolphins and ravens) possess a certain level of sense of identity. The species listed in parentheses have passed the so-called *mirror test*, that is, they pay specific attention to colored spots painted on their body when they look at them in a mirror; such response means that they recognize themselves. The level of identity the test captures is indeed elementary; furthermore, there is no academic consensus on the validity of this assessment.

[18] Pinker, Steven. *How the Mind Works*. New York: W. W. Norton & Company, Inc., 1997.

[19] **The seat of mind**: The human brain consists of four structures: cerebral cortex, limbic system, cerebellum and brain stem. The sentence of this quote can be further refined: "The mind is what the cerebral cortex does and the cerebral cortex of other mammals cannot do." To say "the mind is what the pre-frontal cortex does...." is even more accurate. The pre-frontal cortex is the seat of key functions of the mind, such as awareness, thought, speech and consciousness. The substantial difference in total weight of human brains and other anthropoid apes' brains resides in the weight of the cerebral cortex.

[20] Lovgren, Stefan. "Chimps, Humans 96 Percent the Same, Gene Study Finds": *National Geographic,* August 31, 2005. Other references use similar percentages; regardless the figure, the fact is that, genetically speaking, humans and chimpanzees are very close.

[21] **The seat of the mind in ancient times**: According to ancient Buddhism, the heart is the organ of the mind. Several Greek philosophers, including Aristotle, also thought that mental function resided in the heart; Greek thinkers, however, did not consider the mind to be a sense.

[22] **Five senses**: The five-sense categorization is attributed to Aristotle. Balance, motion, time and temperature, among others, are some of the candidate senses to add to the standard list.

[23] **Mind as a sense**: The consideration of the mind as a sense, a categorization exclusive of Buddhism, is holistic and eliminates the body-mind dichotomy. Such integration also puts an end to the divider between physical illnesses and mental disorders; every disease would be, by nature, physical in its origins.

[24] **The oldest sense in evolution**: Plants, which lack sensory organs, do smell one another. Botanists are now learning how this primitive sense works. Chamovitz, Daniel. "What a Plant Smells": *Scientific American,* Volume 306, Number 5, May 2012.

[25] Damasio, Antonio. "How the Brain Creates Mind": *Scientific American,* Volume 12, Number 1, December 1999.

[26] **Age of consciousness**: The first traces of consciousness might have appeared in remote anthropoid apes five to seven million years ago. Chimpanzees, which as a species are some six million years old and share a common ancestor with humans, display behaviors with superior expressions of consciousness when compared to other mammals.

[27] **Materiality of existence**: The characteristic of materiality establishes the physicality of all the expressions of human existence; there are no immaterial or metaphysical entities within or besides the human body. For us, human beings, it is hard to understand the paradoxical nature of our physical and symbolic identities. There is, however, a wide agreement among modern

scientists—biologists, neurologists, geneticists—that life and consciousness are material phenomena.

[28] **Reincarnation and rebirth:** There is no way to restore a working version of our self (our symbolic identity) in another structure, as we can do with computer data and software when we transfer them to a new machine. The Hindu theory of reincarnation suggests that the self or soul may reenter another body which, depending upon the actions in current or previous lives, will be a higher- or lower-level body. In Buddhism there is no self or soul that reincarnates in another body; instead, a selfless stream of consciousness moves from being to being. Buddhist scholars compare such a stream with the flame of a wood log that moves on to fire up a new log. This book does not subscribe to the beliefs in reincarnation or rebirth; they are unrelated to the notions of anxiety-and-stress and inner harmony.

[29] **Half-animal and half-symbolic**: The notions of physical individuality and symbolic identity originate from American anthropologist Ernest Becker's book *The Denial of Death,* already referenced. The expression half-animal and half-symbolic comes from German philosopher Erich Fromm, again through *The Denial of Death.* "The reason why the old core of man—his *essence,* something fixed in his nature—was never found," says Ernest Becker, quoting Erich Fromm, "was that there was no essence, that the essence of man is really his *paradoxical nature,* the fact that he is half-animal and half-symbolic."

[30] **Characteristics of human existence**: The three characteristics—impermanence, materiality of mental phenomena and predisposition to suffering—are the entrance door to the Buddha's teachings. The scope and sequence of the three characteristics in Buddhist literature are somewhat different to what is discussed here. In Buddhist doctrine, the characteristics apply to all phenomena, not only to human existence. Furthermore,

what this book sometimes calls *predisposition to suffering* in humans, the teachings consider *plain* suffering in all phenomena. The sequence of the characteristics in Buddhist texts is impermanence, suffering and materiality; the sequence in this text is materiality, impermanence and predisposition to suffering.

[31] **Inner Harmony**: An inner state that permits us to be at peace and act confidently even in the face of difficulties. Inner harmony is synonymous with inner peace; this author prefers the former expression because inner peace is commonly associated with religious practices or spiritual states. The closest to *inner harmony* in Pali is *nibbana*. Literally, *nibbana* means the extinction, cessation or explosion of something that disappears, which, in the context of the third truth, is suffering.

[32] *Majjhima Nikaya* 10: *Satipatthana Sutta: The Foundations of Mindfulness.*

[33] **The foundations of mindfulness**: The foundations of mindfulness, also known as the framework or the establishments of mindfulness, are four items. Besides body, sensations and mental states, they also include *dhamma*, the essence of the Buddha's teachings. The Sage presents the foundations in two discourses, namely, *Majjhima Nikaya* 10: *Satipatthana Sutta: The Foundations of Mindfulness,* and *Digha Nikaya* 22: *Mahasatipatthana Sutta: The Great Foundations of Mindfulness.*

[34] Rodriguez, Tory. "What Just Happened": *Scientific American Mind,* November/December 2011.

[35] Thoreau, Henry D. *Walden: A Fully Annotated Edition.* New Haven, CT: Yale University Press, 2004.

[36] **Designer of mindfulness meditation**: The techniques of mindfulness meditation, the documentation of which is in the Pali Canon, are very old; the Buddha himself seems to have been the developer of these techniques twenty-five centuries ago.

[37] **Guidelines for meditation**: Most types of meditation have in common the four elements presented in the body of the text, which exclude practices that might involve sounds (as chants or mantras), or motions (as dances or ritualistic gestures). The National Center for Complementary and Alternative Medicine at the American National Institute of Health considers these guidelines as the key points in the practice of meditation.

[38] **Sensations around the breath as an anchor**: The breath-sensations duo as a spot to focus attention does not appear in any of the translations of the *Satipatthana Sutta: The Foundations of Mindfulness* that this author has reviewed. The translation of the *Mahasatipatthana Sutta, The Great Discourse on Steadfast Mindfulness*, by U Jotika and U Dhamminda, however, describes this anchor in a footnote. The Vipassana Meditation organization, which has numerous centers throughout the world, teaches a meditation technique that focuses attention on the sensations around the breath. This technique is the entry-point of their ten-day mindfulness meditation courses.

[39] *Anguttara Nikaya* 9.64: *Nivarana Sutta: Hindrances.*

[40] **Negative critique of meditation**: Indian thinker Krishnamurti Jiddhu, an advocate of the passive, choiceless awareness as the key element in our path toward understanding, is a sharp critic of meditation techniques that require the focusing of attention on mental or physical devices such as mantras or rosaries.

[41] **Meditation increases gray matter density**: There have been a number of research projects on the effects of meditation in the brain and its functions. One of them, a controlled study on subjects who meditated daily for eight weeks, identified changes in gray-matter density in areas of the brain, such as the hippocampus, that are associated with memory, empathy and sense of self. They also found a reduction of gray matter in the amygdala, a region connected to stress and anxiety. A control group did not show any of these changes. Bhanoo, Sindya N. "How

Meditation May Change the Brain." *The New York Times* (Health & Science), January 28, 2011, retrieved July 14, 2012.

[42] Santa Teresa de Jesús. *La vida de la Santa Madre Teresa de Jesús, y algunas de las mercedes que Dios le hizo, escritas por ella misma.* (Saint Theresa of Jesus. *The Life of Saint Theresa of Jesus and some of the Mercies that God Gave Her Written by Herself.*) Website: Biblioteca virtual Miguel de Cervantes. Retrieved December 29, 2006.

[43] **Harmful and wholesome mental states**: The absence of harmful mental states does not imply the presence of a reciprocal wholesome state. Since mental states are blurred and ambiguous, they do not always have clear-cut opposites. Still there are some unambiguous, opposing duos such as avarice-generosity, attachment-detachment, jealousy-trust, anger-calm, hatred-love, disgust-charm, partiality-impartiality, fanaticism-tolerance, and chauvinism-fairness.

[44] **Emotions originating in the brain**: Emotions and sensory signals generally, but not always, occur in the body. An example of an exception is the emotional state that might result from recalling past circumstances during which we became, for example, angry or frightened. The recollection of these circumstances, which obviously occur in the brain, might bring back the emotions we felt the first time. We might even clench fists or get pale again, events that happen in the body; still these recalled emotions start in the brain.

[45] **The eightfold path**: The eightfold path, the Buddha's fourth truth, is a set of eight habits or practices that make up his expanded recipe to end suffering. In the Pali Canon, the word *right* precedes the denomination of each habit. Each of the Pali denominations has several English translations; a typical translation of the eight items is right view, right thought, right speech, right action, right livelihood, right effort, right mindfulness and right concentration. This book's denominations parallel the Buddha's eightfold path. Though they are overall

equivalent, the words used here do not coincide with those listed above; the choice of words is as follows: mindful view, mindful thought, mindful speech, mindful action, mindful livelihood, determination, mindfulness and mindfulness meditation.

[46] **Determination or right effort and SWOT analysis**: The four avenues of determination present an interesting resemblance to a management methodology known as SWOT analysis (the strengths, weaknesses, opportunities and threats that exist in the internal and external environments of an organization). The application of the SWOT analysis aims at the utilization of the strengths, the correction of the weaknesses, the lucrative use of the opportunities, and the control of the threats. The practice of determination (or right effort) is the application of a kind of SWOT analysis in our battle against suffering. Within such parallel, we should: (1) Reinforce the application of the wholesome qualities (strengths) that we know we have and are already using successfully. (2) Stay away from damaging circumstances we know as such and avoid the application of unwholesome traits we possess (weaknesses). (3) Apply the wholesome qualities we have as well as the favorable circumstances that surround us (opportunities), and from which we have not benefited yet. (4) Avoid harmful qualities and circumstances that could increase our suffering (threats) though they are not yet active.

[47] *Matthew 7:12. Luke 6:31* also contains a very similar text: "Do to others as you would have them do to you."

[48] *Khuddaka Nikaya: Sutta Nipata* III.11, *Nalaka Sutta: To Nalaka.*

[49] *Khuddaka Nikaya: Dhammapada 129-130: The Path of the Teachings 129-130.*

[50] Thich Nhat Hanh. *The Heart of the Buddha's Teaching: Transforming Suffering into Peace, Joy and Liberation.* Berkeley, California: Broadway Books, 1999.

[51] *Khuddaka Nikaya: Dhammapada 1-2: The Path of the Teachings 1-2.*

[52] *Khuddaka Nikaya: Dhammapada 3-5: The Path of the Teachings 3-5.*

[53] *Khuddaka Nikaya: Dhammapada 133-134: The Path of the Teachings 133-134.*

[54] *Majjhima Nikaya* 10: *Satipatthana Sutta. The Foundations of Mindfulness.*

[55] **Free will**: Free will is our theoretical ability to make conscious choices. According to recent neuroscientific research, the actual existence of such a human trait is uncertain. Different studies conclude that many actions that we think we are making consciously, such as choosing the color to come out in a roulette toss, happen somewhere in our subconscious mind before we make our *conscious* selection. Using encephalograms, neurophysiologist Benjamin Liber did the pioneering work in this area at the University of California, San Francisco. Several experiments with newer imaging technology have confirmed the original conclusions.

[56] **Brain usage by senses**: Vision uses about 30 percent of the brain cortex; touch, some 8 percent; and hearing, just three percent. Grady, Denis. "The Vision Thing: Mainly in the Brain": *Discover*, June 1993.

[57] **Homeostatic imbalance**: Homeostatic imbalance is the inability of our organism to adjust to *normal* disruptions. Though homeostatic imbalance may originate in some pathological disorders, the aging process is the main culprit of such imbalance.

[58] **Suffering and stress**: Thanissaro Bhikkhu (Geoffrey DeGraff), an American Buddhist monk and scholar, considers

the word *stress* as the most appropriate English translation for *dukkha,* the Pali word for suffering. One of the most profuse Buddhist writers and Pali Canon translators, Thanissaro Bhikkhu is a respected authority in the Buddhist academy.

[59] **Meditation as an exercise of inhibitory circuits**: The strengthening of inhibitory circuits through mindfulness meditation is a not-yet tested hypothesis. Neuroscientist Jason Shumake, PhD, University of Texas at Austin, reviewed this hypothesis as described in Appendix 4. As expressed in a personal communication, Doctor Shumake considers it reasonable to think that inhibitory circuits can be strengthened, "as it fits with the energy dynamics of the 'use it or lose it principle,' which works at many different levels in the body, from cells to muscles."

[60] Zimmer, Carl. "Stop Paying Attention: Zoning Out Is a Crucial Mental State": *Discover,* June 2009.

[61] **Sense of belonging**: With some variations, the sense of belonging is also referred to as a sense of community, affiliation and togetherness, among several other equivalent denominations.

[62] **Sociability as a survival advantage**: In remote ages, we could hypothesize, solitary and morose individuals had fewer opportunities to obtain food through collective hunting and to meet sex partners. Sociable individuals, consequently, had better chances to survive and leave offspring. We, the majority of modern people, may have as an inborn predisposition some kind of appetite for belonging to some group, and some kind of aversion to solitude.

[63] *Majjhima Nikaya* 10: *Satipatthana Sutta: The Foundations of Mindfulness.*

[64] **Rhythms of brain activity**: The frequency of the human brain activity, measured in cycles per second, is determined through electro-encephalographic (EEG) technology. During

normal waking conditions, that frequency (*beta rhythm* is the medical term that describes it) is between 12 and 30 cycles per second. Other rhythms include alpha (8–12 cycles per second), theta (4–7), delta (0.1–4), and gamma (30–100). Alpha rhythm characterizes relaxation states as meditation; theta rhythm manifests in drowsy, light sleeping and deep meditation states; and delta rhythm shows during deep sleep. There is no scientific agreement on the conditions associated with gamma frequency. Any state that deviates significantly from the beta rhythm is an altered state of consciousness.

[65] **The Theosophical Society**: The Theosophical Society is a worldwide organization that aims to awakening human wisdom and understanding of the mysteries of the universe. The existence of spiritual masters, with whom *advanced* humans can get in touch, is a prominent postulate of theosophy, a speculative study of the nature of Divinity.

[66] Lutyens, Mary. *Krishnamurti: The Years of Awakening*. New York: Avon Books, 1975.

[67] **Sri Krishna**: A deity worshipped in India, comparable with Jesus of Nazareth in Christianity.

[68] **Lord Maitreya**: A future reincarnation of Buddha, according to several old traditions.

[69] **Saint Theresa's mystical experiences**: As documented in her writings, Saint Theresa, during her formative years, feels that Jesus Christ does converse with her. At other times, she feels that her body is actually levitating. These psychical phenomena have neurological explanation: Under deep autosuggestion, the peripheral nervous system sends to the brain clear signals that these events are actually taking place; they become truly unambiguous in the case of the saint. In such situations, the perceived experiences tend to confirm beliefs, beliefs reinforce faith (and the intensity of autosuggestion) and faith, further strengthened, facilitates the repetition of similar experiences.

[70] **Poor in self**: An interpretation of the first Christian Beatitude ("Blessed are the poor in spirit for theirs is the kingdom of heaven," *Matthew 5:3*) suggests that Jesus actually meant, "Blessed the poor in self," that is, blessed those whose self is small. This interpretation is worthy of note because the term *self* in Pali (*atta*) also means *soul* or *spirit*.

[71] **Use of first person singular pronoun**: The use of first person singular pronouns is discouraged not only by guidelines of good writing but also by inspirational writers and motivational speakers. The use of *I* or *me* (as well as *my* and *mine*) is considered presumptuous and divisive. Are these usages a reflection of large redundant egos? Any answer to this question is hypothetical. Indian thinker J. Krishnamurti, supposedly an *egoless* person, consistently used to refer to himself in his talks as the *speaker*.

[72] **What we lose through meditation**: This story appears in the Foreword of *The Dhammapada*, translated for the Modern Reader by Eknath Easwand. In the story, the teacher answering the questions is the Buddha himself. While keeping the emphasis of the message, the narrative is rephrased because this text does not seem to correspond to any actual document in the Pali Canon.

[73] Abraham Maslow. *Motivation and Personality*. New York: Harper & Row Publishers Inc., 1987.

[74] *The Verses on the Faith Mind* (Hsin Hsin Ming). This text, less than eleven hundred words long in English, is attributed to Seng-Tsan, a sixth century Chinese Zen patriarch. The wording differences of the English versions reflect the difficulties of translations from Eastern languages; the spirit and beauty of the message, however, stay in all versions. The lines as quoted are adapted to the terminology this book uses, without altering the essence of their meaning.

[75] **The Path, the Way or the Tao**: Instead of *Path*, the translations of *The Verses on the Faith Mind* use either the English word *Way* or the Chinese word *Tao,* which means *Absolute Principle* or *Natural Order* and is the originating root of the word *Taoism*. Taoism is a Chinese mystical philosophy that advocates a simple honest life and no interference with the course of natural events in order to conform to the Tao. The Taoist philosophy evolved into a religion with much magical content. The choice of *Path,* a synonym of *Way*, aims at consistency with the *Path of Mindfulness* that the Buddha recommends. Furthermore, for the third line, most translations use *love and hatred* instead of *cravings and aversions,* as chosen for this book.

[76] **Body and sensations' anchors not to use**: Meditation should be as simple as possible. Though the following recommendation is for every practitioner, beginners must certainly avoid experimenting with additional anchors such as other parts of the body (as the navel or the area between the eyebrows), other functions of the body (as heartbeats or the belly's ups and downs as we breathe in and breathe out), or other sensations (such as the sensation of the air going through our throat). These not-to-use examples frequently appear in the instructions of other meditation techniques. If experienced meditators find that other approaches are improving their faculty of awareness, they might use the *proscribed* techniques, as long as their practice does not involve or develop any kind of attachment.

[77] **Vipassana Meditation Centers**: The Vipassana Meditation Centers set a leading example of absence of financial gains in their training programs; these centers are organizations that offer Vipassana meditation courses as taught by S. N. Goenka and his assistant teachers. Vipassana is a mindfulness meditation technique in the tradition of Sayagyi U Ba Khin, a notable teacher from Burma (today Myanmar). S. N. Goenka, born in Myanmar of Indian ancestry, learned Vipassana from Sayagyi U Ba Khin. After mastering the technique, he has led the crea-

tion of more than one hundred Vipassana Meditation Centers throughout the world. The training programs at these centers are free of charge either for the course or for the lodging and boarding during retreats. All Vipassana Meditation Centers are supported by voluntary donations of people who want to contribute for future courses, and by voluntary work of all teachers as well as the staff and support personnel. There are no charges for courses, not even to cover the cost of food or accommodation. Donations made by people at the end of each course, after they experience the benefits of Vipassana, go toward paying the expenses of future students.

[78] **Meditation circles**: The practitioners of meditation, as this author interprets what Buddhist scholars call the three jewels, should take three refuges; meditation circles, the third one, is one of them. The three refuges are (1) refuge in their essential self (the Buddha nature we all possess), (2) refuge in the Buddha's teachings (the basic laws of Nature), and (3) refuge in a meditation circle (the community, which refers to a circle of friends, for secular people, or a community of monks, for those who opt for a secluded life).

[79] **Meditative states, or absorptions**: The description of the four meditative states, which is only some two hundred words long, appears, with different levels of detail, in several of the Buddha's discourses (e.g., *Digha Nikaya* 22: *Mahasatipatthana Sutta: The Great Foundations of Mindfulness*). The narratives, in general, are very abstract. Furthermore, there are several translations of every discourse and even more interpretations provided by non–Pali speaking authors (as this author). The differences between the different translations and interpretations plus the subjective nature of all mental experiences make impossible a clear-cut understanding of the four meditative states. Meditators must not try to follow the interpretation of this book (or the understanding of anybody else). As they gain experience in meditation, however, the meditative states will progressively make increasing sense for every student.

[80] **Another perspective on the four meditative levels**: The following quote should shed light on these ambiguous states (at the risk of adding confusion). Romanian historian of religions Mircea Eliade, an authorized scholar of Indian religions, defines the four meditative states as follows: "(1) to purify the mind from the *temptations* (of the hindrances)—that is to isolate the mind from external agents; in short, to obtain an initial autonomy of consciousness; (2) to suppress the dialectical functions of the mind, obtain concentration, and perfect mastery of a rarified consciousness; (3) to suspend all relations with both the sensible world and with memory, and to obtain a placid lucidity without any other content than *consciousness of existing*; (4) to reintegrate the *opposites* and obtain the bliss of *pure awareness.*" Eliade, Mircea. *Yoga: Immortality and Freedom*. New York, NY: Bollingen Foundation Inc., 1958.

[81] **Two stages of mindfulness meditation**: The seventh and eighth habits of the Buddha's eightfold path—mindfulness and meditation—suggest two different forms of meditation. Such differentiation is included in this author's previous book in Spanish *Hacia el Buda desde el occidente* (*To the Buddha from the West,* presently not available in English). This separation seems unnecessary. As meditators gain experience in their practice, they will experience that, in spite of these two well-defined stages and the variety of meditation instructions, mindfulness meditation is one single whole.

[82] "Dōgen," Wikiquote, http://en.wikiquote.org/wiki/Dōgen, retrieved August 8, 2012.

[83] Jiddhu, Krishnamurti. *The First & Last Freedom*. New York: Harper & Row Publishers, Inc., 1954.

[84] **Krishnamurti's mindfulness**: Krishnamurti does not use the word *mindfulness*; instead, he uses the word *meditation* in the sense of mindfulness, as defined in this book. The Hindu philosopher denigrates of all mental concentration techniques, particularly if they work on artificial devices such as prayers, man-

tras or figures. To avoid confusion, the wordings of the Krishnamurti's quoted texts are changed accordingly.

[85] Jiddhu, Krishnamurti. *Freedom from the Known*. Lutyens, Mary, editor. New York: Harper Collins Publishers, 1975.

[86] **The original quote on a master in the art of living**: "A master in the art of living draws no sharp distinction between his work and his play, his labor and his leisure, his mind and his body, his education and his recreation. He hardly knows which is which. He simply pursues his vision of excellence through whatever he is doing and leaves others to determine whether he is working or playing. To himself he always seems to be doing both. Enough for him that he does it well." Lawrence Pearsall Jacks: *Education through Recreation*: *Quote Investigator, Dedicated to Tracing Quotations*. http://quoteinvestigator.com/2010/08/27/master, retrieved August 27, 2012.

[87] Dostoyevsky, Fyodor. *Devils (The Possessed)*. Ware, Hertfordshire, England: Wordsworth Editions Ltd., 2010.

[88] *Majjhima Nikaya* 22: *Alagaddupama Sutta: The Simile of the Snake.*

[89] *Majjhima Nikaya* 10: *Satipatthana Sutta*: *The Foundations of Mindfulness.*

[90] *Digha Nikaya* 22: *Satipatthana Sutta*: *The Great Foundations of Mindfulness.*

[91] **Meditation in the Buddha's teachings**: The word *meditation*, with the connotation in this book, does not appear in the teachings. The Buddha's guidelines for mindfulness focused on the breath is the only reference in the Pali Canon's Division of Discourses (as far as this author knows) about a monk (or a meditator) sitting down with legs crossed and the body erect; this practice is the entry point to meditation. By extension, the directions to focus mindfulness on sensations, performed in a

sitting position, fit quite well within the definition of meditation.

[92] **The six internal and the six external sense-spheres**: In Buddhist doctrine, the set of six pairs—eyes-forms, ears-sounds, nose-odors, tongue-flavors, body sensory system-tangibles, brain-mental objects—are the sense-spheres. The sense organs correspond to the six internal sense spheres; their associated objects are called the six external ones. These six pairs are the means or domain of the mental processes. The six organ senses and their six corresponding objects act as intermediary between outer and inner phenomena, on one hand, and cognition, the fifth aggregate of personality, on the other. The internal and external sense-spheres emphasize the importance in every experience of both the external objects and their associated sensory signals generated by the contact between each pair. Appetites and fears do not originate in the sense-spheres; they actually result from the generated mental formations, the fourth aggregate of personality.

[93] **Meditator versus monk**: The Buddha's discourses are always addressed to monks; in this Appendix, the words *meditator* or *meditators* replace *monk* or *monks*.

[94] **Denominations of mental states' areas**: The section on mental states explains the application of attention to eight mental states' areas described as desires or greed, fears or hatred, delusion, lethargy, openness, realization, concentration and freedom. The subtitles used in this section do not appear in the original texts.

[95] **Mindfulness meditation**: Most translators of the Buddha discourses refer to the eighth practice of the eightfold path as "right concentration."

[96] **List of authors, scholars and religious figures quoted or mentioned in this book:**

Ajaan Maha Bua	Fromm, Erich	Saint Theresa of Jesus
Analayo	Goenka, S. N.	Sayagyi U Ba Khin
Ananda Maitreya	Grady, Denis	Seng-Tsan
Aristotle	Jacks, Lawrence P.	Shumake, Jason
Becker, Ernest	Jesus of Nazareth	Siddhattha Gotama
Bhanoo, Sindya N.	Krishnamurti, J.	Soma Thera
Bhikkhu Bodhi	Lord Maitreya	Sri Krishna
Buddha, the	Lovgren, Stefan	Sun Tzu
Byrom, Thomas	Lutyens, Mary	Thanissaro Bhikkhu
Chamovitz, Daniel	Maslow, Abraham	Thich Nhat Hanh
Damasio, Antonio	Mathew, Apostle	Thoreau, Henry D.
Darwin, Charles	Michelangelo	U Dhamminda
Dōgen, Eihei	Ñanamoli Bhikkhu	U Jotika
Dostoevsky, Fyodor	Nyanasatta Thera	Walshe, Maurice
Easwand, Eknath	Pinker, Steven	Zimmer, Carl
Eliade, Mircea	Rodriguez, Tory